D02S2929

SINGAPORE
ENCOUNTER

JOSHUA SAMUEL BROWN
MAT OAKLEY

Singapore Encounter

Published by Lonely Planet Publications Pty Ltd
ABN 36 005 607 983

Australia	Head Office, Locked Bag 1,
	Footscray, Victoria 3011
	☎ 03 8379 8000 fax 03 8379 8111
	talk2us@lonelyplanet.com.au
USA	150 Linden St, Oakland, CA 94607
	☎ 510 250 6400
	toll free 800 275 8555
	fax 510 893 8572
	info@lonelyplanet.com
UK	2nd fl, 186 City Rd
	London EC1V 2NT
	☎ 020 7106 2100 fax 020 7106 2101
	go@lonelyplanet.co.uk

This title was commissioned in Lonely Planet's
Melbourne office and produced by: **Commissioning
Editors** Shawn Low, Ilaria Walker, Tashi Wheeler
Coordinating Editor Nigel Chin **Cartographer** Andras
Bogdanovits **Coordinating Layout Designer** Frank Deim
Managing Editors Bruce Evans, Liz Heynes **Managing
Cartographer** Corey Hutchison **Managing Layout
Designer** Celia Wood **Cover and Internal Image
Researcher** Aude Vauconsant, lonelyplanetimages
.com **Thanks to** Errol Hunt, Indra Kilfoyle, Lisa Knights,
Kirsten Rawlings

Cover photograph Paragon Shopping Centre decorated
with lantern for Chinese New Year, Richard l'Anson/Lonely
Planet Images. **Internal photographs** p45, p63, p72,
p95, p109, p139 by Joshua Samuel Brown; all other
photographs by Lonely Planet Images and by Felix Hug
except p138, p140 Glenn Beanland, p16 Mervin Chua, p24
Alain Evrard, p6 Manfred Gottschalk, p26 Susan Storm and
p30, p173 Phil Weymouth.

All images are copyright of the photographers unless
otherwise indicated. Many of the images in this guide
are available for licensing from **Lonely Planet Images:**
www.lonelyplanetimages.com.

ISBN 978 1 74179 678 0

10 9 8 7 6 5 4 3

Printed by Hang Tai Printing Company, Hong Kong.
Printed in China.

HOW TO USE THIS BOOK
Colour-Coding & Maps
Colour-coding is used for symbols on maps and in
the text that they relate to (eg all eating venues on
the maps and in the text are given a green knife and
fork symbol). Each neighbourhood also gets its own
colour, and this is used down the edge of the page
and throughout that neighbourhood section.

Prices
Multiple prices listed with reviews (eg €10/5 or
€10/5/20) indicate adult/child, adult/concession
or adult/child/family.

---

*Although the authors and Lonely Planet have taken
all reasonable care in preparing this book, we make
no warranty about the accuracy or completeness of
its content and, to the maximum extent permitted,
disclaim all liability arising from its use.*

Send us your feedback We love to hear from
readers – your comments help make our books better. We read every word you send us, and we always
guarantee that your feedback goes straight to the
appropriate authors. The most useful submissions are
rewarded with a free book. To send us your updates
and find out about Lonely Planet events, newsletters
and travel news visit our award-winning website:
lonelyplanet.com/contact.

Note: We may edit, reproduce and incorporate
your comments in Lonely Planet products such as
guidebooks, websites and digital products, so let us
know if you don't want your comments reproduced or
your name acknowledged. For a copy of our privacy
policy visit **lonelyplanet.com/privacy**.

MIX
Paper from
responsible sources
FSC™ C021741
www.fsc.org

JOSHUA SAMUEL BROWN

Joshua Samuel Brown (otherwise known as Josambro) is an American-born expatriate currently living a professionally nomadic lifestyle. A prolific traveller and writer, his features have appeared in an eclectic variety of publications around the globe, including the *South China Morning Post, Business Traveller Asia, Clamor Magazine* and *Cat Fancy*. Joshua's debut book, *Vignettes of Taiwan*, offers tales of betel nut beauties and how to avoid jail time by impersonating a Mormon. To date, Joshua has

co-authored five travel guides for Lonely Planet, keeps a regular blog called *Snarky Tofu* at josambro.blogspot.com and also writes slightly more serious stuff at www.josambro.com. Joshua was also a 2009 USC Annenberg/Getty Arts Journalism Fellow.

JOSHUA'S THANKS

Thanks to Tony Tan, my Singaporean Tenzing Norgay, without whom I wouldn't have found half of the cool stuff I found, or eaten half the great food I ate. Thanks to Dawn, Ginny, Colin and Ruqxana for mental support, and to Jon, Asako, Sam and Hannah as always for giving me a place to stay. Special gratitude to Dr Matthew Herd, podiatrist extraordinaire, for helping me to walk straighter.

THE PHOTOGRAPHER

Felix Hug used to shoot hoops for a professional basketball team in Switzerland before he decided that shooting images was more enjoyable. In 2007 Felix was the runner-up at the Travel Photographer of the Year awards. He received an honourable mention at the *PDN/National Geographic Traveler* 'World in Focus' contest in 2005 and took home the *Asian Geographic* Nikon Grand Prize in 2004. Felix believes that the job of the travel photographer is to capture inspiring images instead of just documenting reality: 'Positive images and compassion will inspire and change the way we look at things.'

Our readers Many thanks to the travellers who wrote to us with helpful hints, useful advice and interesting anecdotes:
Allan Cowin

Laid-back Clarke Quay comes alive at night thanks to an assortment of bars, clubs and restaurants

CONTENTS

THIS IS SINGAPORE

Once sullenly wary of outsiders, Singapore is now screaming its name to the world. Once upon a time they stopped longhairs at the border, now they're offering them big salaries to run digital animation labs. Once upon a time the city frowned on late nights, alcohol and wanton frivolity, now it's one of the nightlife capitals of Asia.

Once upon a time in Singapore... The fairy tales still get told of social controls so obsessively, surreally punctilious they achieved global infamy. Yes, it's still illegal to chew gum (without prescription!) and jaywalk, and yes the government still fusses, prods and badgers its citizens in every single aspect of their lives, but the 'Fine' city has actually transcended the joke and become, yes, a fine city.

At the centre of it all, the Colonial District is its cultural heart, home to some of Asia's most outstanding museums, some of its grandest Victorian architecture and, providing a spiky counterpoint, the unforgettable Esplanade theatre overlooking Marina Bay. Singapore's economic lifeblood used to flow through that bay and up the river. Now the shadow of a new economy looms over it, as the giant Sands casino resort rises towards full completion, while a barrage has turned the bay into a reservoir that will be the centrepiece for the New Singapore: globally minded, affluent and fun.

Upstream, echoes of the past cling to the river bank, but the belch and clatter of bumboat commerce has given way to the belch and clatter of drinkers and diners, as businesspeople mingle with mall-weary tourists over a few sundowners before taking on some of the city's superb clubs and restaurants. And everywhere, from fancy French cuisine to the ubiquitous hawker stalls, is food, the one defining obsession that unites everyone, if only momentarily. Any visitor willing to throw themselves into this food paradise will find no quicker way into the soul of Singapore.

Top Another exciting night of live music (p165) in Singapore **Bottom** The durian-like Esplanades – Theatres on the Bay (p67) adds a distinctive architectural flavour to Singapore's skyline

>HIGHLIGHTS

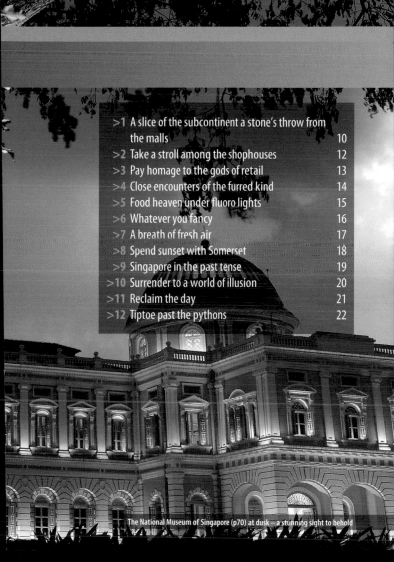

The National Museum of Singapore (p70) at dusk – a stunning sight to behold

>1 LITTLE INDIA

A SLICE OF THE SUBCONTINENT A STONE'S THROW FROM THE MALLS

Many parts of Singapore have been trampled by shopping centres – a process of mall-ification that has robbed entire areas of their sense of place. Little India is one of the happy exceptions and for our money there is nowhere in Singapore that matches it for street atmosphere, especially at night.

Little India teems with life – it's hard to believe you're just a few minutes from Orchard Rd – and the greatest pleasure is wandering around to soak it all up: the countless places to eat, the gold shops filled with haggling families from India, the garland sellers, CD shops thumping bhangra and the dozens of smells, both good and bad. While many areas of the city die after dark, there always seems to be activity on the streets of Little India, which light up spectacularly in October for the Deepavali festival.

Serangoon Rd forms the spine of the district, but it's the lanes on either side that warrant the most exploring. Next to the pungent wet market, hawker centre and 1st-floor sari shops of Tekka Centre (p90), Buffalo Rd's open-air vegetable stalls bustle around the clock, spilling detritus onto the street as shoppers shuffle along the five-foot-ways lined with bags plump with okra, eggplants and more. There's something refreshingly grubby and un-Singaporean about it all.

Race Course Rd is thick with food shops, including the famous Banana Leaf Apolo (p91), where diners sweat over fiery fish-head curry every night. Around the Dunlop St and Dickson Rd area are more eateries, handicraft shops, hostels and the Prince of Wales pub (p94).

At the other end of Serangoon Rd is the notorious Mustafa Centre (p89), a 24-hour shopping behemoth crammed with every known retailable item on earth and, it sometimes seems, every person too.

>2 CHINATOWN
TAKE A STROLL AMONG THE SHOPHOUSES

It might seem strange to have a Chinatown in a city dominated by ethnic Chinese, but this district of narrow lanes and once-crumbling shophouses was the area Sir Stamford Raffles demarcated in his segregated Singapore town plan for the Chinese immigrants.

The area is still rich in history – and the first stop for any new visitor should be the Chinatown Heritage Centre (p51), which portrays the district's squalid past. It's hard to imagine, now that the renovators have swarmed all over the place and filled it with boutique hotels and fashionable restaurants. Pockets of old Chinatown still remain in streets such as Keong Saik Rd and Chinatown Complex.

Pagoda, Temple, Smith and Trengganu Sts are the tourist traps, riddled with market stalls (and a great night food market) and bookended by two important religious sites: the Hindu Sri Mariamman Temple (p51) and newly built Buddha Tooth Relic Temple (p51).

Cross South Bridge Rd and enter Club St, once home to many clan associations headquarters, now a magnet for fashionable businesses and restaurants. Over the top of Ann Siang Hill are Amoy and Telok Ayer Sts, home of the Thian Hock Keng temple (p54), an area that heaves with lunching office workers during the day, but is almost deserted at night.

>3 ORCHARD ROAD
PAY HOMAGE TO THE GODS OF RETAIL

Orchard Rd was once a leafy boulevard lined with plantations (hence the name). These days, though, Singapore's money doesn't grow on trees; it's harvested in malls – and nowhere do they grow more thickly than here. The sheer scale of this retail barrage can be oppressive and overwhelming, particularly for reluctant shoppers (in other words, men). On weekends and in holiday seasons, the pavements are often so packed that walking is reduced to a shuffle. But there are compensations for those who contemplate with horror a day of gasping at shoes and suffering lathers of indecision over dresses – including the street's many wonderful opportunities for eating and, if you're there during Christmas, the breathtaking light displays.

Orchard Rd and its environs encompass many miniature worlds. Observe the expat wives comparing maid problems over cake at Tanglin Mall (p42) or Paragon (p42), teen fashion molls evaluating the latest Japanese pink fur boots at Far East Plaza (p43), hipsters calculating the cool quotient of a $90 T-shirt at the Heeren (p43), hopeful European men eyeing up the parades of Thai and Filipina girls at Orchard Towers, hopeful Indian men eyeing up the maids who congregate in their thousands at Lucky Plaza on Sundays, or the fussy, bouffanted *tai-tais* (wealthy ladies of leisure) bothering the perfume girls at posh Takashimaya (p42).

HIGHLIGHTS

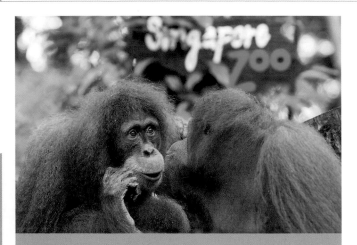

>4 ZOO & NIGHT SAFARI
CLOSE ENCOUNTERS OF THE FURRED KIND

Sometimes the relentless development and redevelopment of Singapore can become tiresome, but not in the case of its world-class zoo and Night Safari (p48), which are forever being upgraded and always for the better. Whatever your opinion of zoos, it can't be denied that the Singapore Zoo has made an excellent job of keeping its animals as happy as possible.

The first creatures you encounter are free-ranging primates: cottontop tamarins, white-faced sakis and siamangs – and there are few places outside Borneo and Sumatra where you can stand under trees with orang-utans a few feet above your head.

Other highlights include the Fragile Forest, a large dome where lemurs and mouse deer scamper across your path, a tree kangaroo lazes in the branches and large flying foxes munch fruit in front of your face.

As evening closes in, the Night Safari next door to the zoo uses open-concept enclosures to get visitors up close with nocturnal creatures such as leopards, free-ranging deer and Malayan tiger.

>5 HAWKER STALLS
FOOD HEAVEN UNDER FLUORO LIGHTS

It is one of the great pleasures of Singapore: ambling into a bustling hawker centre in your flip-flops, picking out a table, wandering among the steam and smoke and chatter of the stalls, then settling down with a few cold beers and stuffing your face. And since almost everything is signed in English, Singapore is one of the most accessible places in Asia to dive into a massive range of regional cuisine.

The traditional favourite for visitors is Newton Circus (p46), which specialises in great seafood, but the touting here can be aggressive. The historical Lau Pa Sat Festival Market (p58) in the CBD is a must-visit – it's been 'upgraded' to 'tourist standard' and many would argue its charm has been lost. In Chinatown, the Smith St Hawker Centre (p61) is a treat, while the Maxwell Rd Hawker Centre (p59) further down the road has a much more local flavour. For a real taste of old-time hawker food where few tourists ever visit, head for Hong Lim Complex (p58) in Chinatown.

For seaside eats, the East Coast Lagoon Food Village (p107) is well-known for its satay stalls and it heaves at night – the perfect spot for a meal and a postprandial stroll along the seashore.

>6 HIGH DINING
WHATEVER YOU FANCY

For many years, Singapore has been in a pitched battle with other countries in the region to cast itself as the food capital of Asia, promoting not only its vibrant (if sometimes sanitised) hawker culture but also its high-end restaurants. There is certainly no shortage of options to lighten your wallet in the name of fine dining, but while the food is frequently top-notch, it has to be said the service in Singapore can leave much to be desired.

Top of the pile for food, service and atmosphere is probably Au Jardin Les Amis (p123) in the Botanic Gardens. Club St also houses several excellent European restaurants, notably L'Angelus (p58) and Senso (p61), while Holland Village's Jalan Merah Saga also contains fine European restaurants such as Original Sin (p124). For fancy Chinese food, locals usually head for big-name restaurants such as Shang Palace (p46) or Royal China (p75), while expat Japanese in Singapore barrel down to Cuppage Plaza for the best taste of home.

>7 SINGAPORE BOTANIC GARDENS

A BREATH OF FRESH AIR

Like all great urban green spaces, entering Singapore's Botanic Gardens (p117) provides instant relief: the roar of traffic melts into the branches and it's easy to forget that you're surrounded by 4.5 million people.

And like most things in Singapore, it's immaculate and well designed. Each area segues into the next, each with its own atmosphere, from the lazy serenity of the Swan Lake to the dense, humid greenery of the rainforest zone to the carefully pruned bonsai and orchid gardens: careful landscaping sits side by side with huge old trees that first poked their heads above ground when Queen Victoria was surveying her Empire.

Of course, visitors don't go hungry. Just inside the Tanglin Gate is a large food court, while the gardens themselves host two of the city's most irresistibly romantic restaurants: Au Jardin Les Amis (p123) and Halia (p123).

Check out the gardens' listing of upcoming events for free tours and the regular free outdoor classical concerts that take place on the Symphony Stage.

>8 RAFFLES HOTEL
SPEND SUNSET WITH SOMERSET

Yes, yes, it's a cliché, but it's also hard to resist the allure of that magnificent ivory frontage, the famous Sikh doorman, the colonial elegance and the echoes of Maugham and Conrad and the days when Singapore was a swampy, dissolute outpost of the British Empire.

Raffles Hotel (p71) started life in 1887 as a modest 10-room bungalow built by the Armenian Sarkies brothers, a far cry from the global brand it has become now, when far more people visit it than sleep in it.

It's best visited in the late afternoon or early evening, when the heat has been sapped from the day, the spotlights bathe the building in romance and the tourists are slightly thinner on the ground, perhaps decanting themselves into the hotel's bars and restaurants.

The Raffles Museum is well worth half an hour. Steer clear of the too-famous Long Bar and slip into a verandah chair at the far more atmospheric Bar & Billiard Room (p76) for an early evening aperitif, followed by one of the best buffets in the city: the incredible, stomach-popping Indian feast laid on nightly in the Tiffin Room (p75).

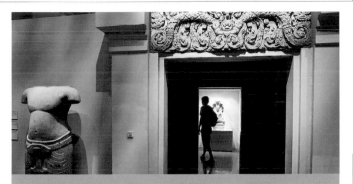

>9 MUSEUMS
SINGAPORE IN THE PAST TENSE

Singapore hosts some of the finest museums in Southeast Asia –
enough to take a week to explore, let alone the average two or three
days most visitors spend here. Most of the best ones are concentrated
in the city centre, which makes it easy to hop between them.

Two Singaporean favourites are the grand Asian Civilisations
Museum (p67), celebrating (naturally) Asian civilisation, and
the charming Peranakan Museum (p70) on Armenian St, which
celebrates local Peranakan culture. The National Museum of Singapore (p70), housed in an architecturally superb Victorian building
and modern annex, is equally magnificent. Close by is the recently
refurbished Singapore Art Museum (p71).

WWII and the Japanese occupation had an enormous impact on
the city, and the experience has been preserved in many laud-
able museums: Fort Siloso on Sentosa (p98), the Battle Box at Fort
Canning Park (p39), Kent Ridge Park's Reflections At Bukit Chandu
(p132), commemorating the Malay Regiment's resistance, Labrador
Park's secret tunnels (p129), the Old Ford Factory (p117), where the
British surrendered, the moving POW memorial at Changi Memorial
& Chapel (p106) and the heartbreaking Kranji War Memorial (p177).
There are also several memorials around the island, including the site
of a Japanese massacre of Chinese civilians at Changi Beach Park.

>10 SENTOSA
SURRENDER TO A WORLD OF ILLUSION

Once a byword for tackiness, Singapore's pleasure isle has been – and continues to be – reborn. Those same blistering beaches of imported sand are still lapped by the oily ocean and thinly shaded by trucked-in palm trees, but the entertainment and eating options have been taken to new heights thanks to the recent opening of the vast new Resorts World hotel-casino, which houses Singapore's own branch of Universal Studios Theme Park.

The Sentosa monorail from Vivocity Mall continues to feed the island with visitors. Speed demons will want to check out the new track at the positively addictive Sentosa Luge (p103). Sure, the ride could be longer, but where else are you going to get the chance to race your friends down to the beach in a vehicle that looks like a baby bath on wheels?

Sun-lovers can plonk themselves under a palm tree, or at one of the Ibiza-inspired bar-restaurants like Café del Mar (p101) or Coastes (p100). More energetic folks might want to check out Wave House (p102), a restaurant-bar boasting not one but two wave pools! History buffs will want to visit Images of Singapore (p98) and the war museum at Fort Siloso (p98), both among the city's better attempts at keeping its past alive.

As the sun sets and the city's weekend beach bunnies migrate to the bars to expose tattoos and tanned flesh, the Songs of the Sea (p99) light-and-sound show entertains those more interested in family-oriented activities.

>11 EAST COAST PARK

RECLAIM THE DAY

Seldom can reclaimed land have been put to such good use. East Coast Park stretches close to 11km and is one of Singapore's most pleasant urban escapes. It's only narrow, but has been superbly designed so that the landscape constantly shifts and changes and the bordering road rarely encroaches on the peace and quiet.

The park offers numerous opportunities for exercise: cycling and rollerblading, wakeboarding and waterskiing at the Ski 360° lagoon (p113), and windsurfing and sailing.

Cycling from the western end to the eastern end, where the planes coming in to land at Changi airport roar directly overhead, and marvelling at the sheer number of ships that anchor offshore is a great way to spend a weekday. During weekends, though, it's too packed to be enjoyable.

And of course it wouldn't be Singapore if there weren't dozens of places to eat and drink, ranging from the wildly popular No Signboard Seafood (p108) to the tiny Mango Tree Indian restaurant (p108) and the outdoor hawker centre at East Coast Lagoon Food Village (p107).

>12 BUKIT TIMAH & MACRITCHIE
TIPTOE PAST THE PYTHONS

If the Botanic Gardens are an admirable exercise in managed vegeta-
tion, then the area officially (and uninspiringly) called the Central Catchment Nature Reserve is a masterpiece of urban wilderness planning.

Bukit Timah Nature Reserve (p117), the highest point on the island
at 163m, is one of only two patches of urban primary rainforest in the
world (the other is in Rio de Janeiro). Though it has been laid with a
concrete path, side trails plunge deep into a forest so rich that one
botanist estimated there are more plant species there than in the
whole of North America.

Linked to Bukit Timah is the MacRitchie Reservoir nature reserve,
which is ringed with dozens of kilometres of trails (see Walking Tour
p146), where walkers can spot macaques, monitor lizards, the occasional python and flying lemur – and walk across the Treetop Walk
suspension bridge – before ending up at the peaceful reservoir park.

>SINGAPORE DIARY

Singapore's rich ethnic brew has resulted in a packed calendar of religious holidays and people of all creeds are encouraged by the city's multicultural masters to participate (though we presume they don't mind if you draw the line at putting skewers through your cheeks). Combine these with annual food, fashion, film, music and shopping events and it becomes pretty difficult to visit Singapore without encountering some festival or other. Before arriving, check the tourism board's excellent online events calendar (www.visitsingapore.com) for the latest.

Singapore is awash with lights and festivities during Chinese New Year (p24)

SINGAPORE DIARY

JANUARY

Ponggal

South Indian harvest festival in mid-January that's heralded with much noise-making – it's customary to cook sweet rice in a pot and let it boil over to symbolise bounty. Place to be: Little India or Sri Mariamman Temple (p51).

Thaipusam

Dramatic Hindu festival featuring acts of masochism. Devotees carry frames attached to their bodies with flesh-piercing skewers and hooks. Place to be: watching the procession from Serangoon Rd to Tank Rd.

FEBRUARY

Chinese New Year

The biggest holiday on the Singapore calendar, marked by lion dancing and brightly decorated trucks carrying drum- and cymbal-bashing men. Families hold open house, unmarried relatives receive *ang pow* (money in red packets) and businesses try to clear their debts. Place to be: Chinatown, of course!

Chingay

www.chingay.org.sg

Huge, vibrant annual street parade and party (usually with undercurrent themes reinforcing social order and racial harmony), held on the

The Chingay parade is a raucous riot of colour and sound

22nd day after Chinese New Year. Formerly on Orchard Rd, but moved to Colonial District in 2008. Buy tickets for viewing galleries, or fight the crowds for vantage points.

MARCH

Mosaic Music Festival

www.mosaicmusicfestival.com

An annual 10-day feast of jazz, funk, hip-hop, world music etc laid on by the Esplanade and sponsored by luminaries like Harry's (a chain of expat pubs), Häagen-Dazs and Heineken. Scores of well-known acts, both local and international, perform at various venues on the Esplanade and there are even free concerts.

APRIL

Qing Ming Festival

Often called All Souls Day, this is when Chinese show gratitude and respect to their ancestors by cleaning and repairing their tombs (or, these days, more likely their urns at the columbarium) and making offerings. Place to be: Kong Meng San Phor Kark See Monastery.

Singapore International Film Festival

www.filmfest.org.sg

Independent and art-house movies are pretty thin on the ground in Hollywood-obsessed Singapore, so this usually excellent festival of world cinema is a rare treat.

World Gourmet Summit

www.worldgourmetsummit.com

Annual gathering of top chefs and celebrities for an orgy of dinners and brunches in the city's top restaurants, as well as wine tastings and cooking master classes.

MAY

Vesak Day

Celebration of Buddha's birth, enlightenment and death through various events, including the releasing of caged birds or other animals to symbolise setting souls free (a practice now actively discouraged since the helpless creatures usually die in the wild). Places to be: Sakaya Muni Buddha Gaya Temple or Buddha Tooth Relic Temple (p51).

JUNE

Great Singapore Sale

www.greatsingaporesale.com.sg

Running from the end of May to the beginning of July (it seems to get longer every year), Orchard Rd and malls are decked with banners, and retailers slash prices. Shoppers' paradise or tourist-board gimmick? Opinions are divided.

Dragon Boat Festival

www.sdba.org.sg

A frenzy of paddling on the Bedok Reservoir in Eastern Singapore. Other dragon-boat events are held throughout the year, including the Singapore River Regatta in November.

Singapore Arts Festival

www.singaporeartsfest.com

Starting in mid-May and ending in mid-June, this annual showcase features dance, music and theatre from Singapore and around the world.

JULY

Singapore Food Festival

www.singaporefoodfestival.com

A month-long celebration of all things edible and Singaporean. Well-known restaurants lay on events and there are cooking classes and food-themed tours for visitors, as well as plenty of opportunities to sample classic Malay, Chinese and Indian dishes.

Chinese opera at the Hungry Ghost Festival

AUGUST

National Day

www.ndp.org.sg

Held on 9 August (rehearsals on the two prior weekends are popular), this huge nationalist frenzy takes all year to prepare and showcases military parades, extravagant civilian processions, Air Force flybys, fervent flag-waving and a concluding fireworks display. Look out for the rows of white-clad People's Action Party (PAP) members.

Hungry Ghost Festival

The day when the souls of the dead are released for feasting and entertainment on earth. The best place to be is probably Chinatown or Geylang, but look for offerings of food left out for the spirits all over the city. Superstitious sorts say the festival month is inauspicious for travelling, but don't let that take the wind out of your sails!

SEPTEMBER

Mooncake Festival

Also known as the Lantern Festival. Sample the namesake cake – traditionally made

The spectacular Thimithi fire-walking ceremony at the Sri Mariamman Temple

with bean paste and duck-egg filling, nowadays mooncakes come in all flavours.

Formula 1 Grand Prix
www.f1singapore.com
Though it's only been going on for a couple of years, the race has already become a massive draw. If you plan to come to town during this period book well in advance.

OCTOBER

Deepavali
The Hindu Festival of Lights sees Little India illuminated by a huge light display for the

entire month and a big street party on the eve of the day itself.

Hari Raya Puasa
Also known as Hari Raya Aidilfitri, this festival celebrates the end of the Ramadan fasting month (it can also occur in September). Place to be: the Arab Quarter for nightly feasts during Ramadan.

NOVEMBER

Thimithi
The mildly frenzied, often raucous Hindu fire-walking festival, when men stroll

PILGRIMAGE TO KUSU

Kusu Island, which means 'Tortoise Island' in Chinese, is normally a tranquil pocket of partly reclaimed land in the Singapore Strait and dotted with trees, picnic benches and small beaches. It houses an attractive Taoist temple to Da Bo Gong (God of Prosperity) and Guan Yin (Goddess of Mercy) and, on top of a prominent central hill, three Malay *kramats* (shrines to saints).

But every year, in the ninth month of the Chinese lunar calendar (some time between late September and November), the island is deluged at weekends with thousands of people, who come to the island on a pilgrimage to pray for wealth, health and good fortune.

According to legend, a magical tortoise spied two drowning sailors – one Malay and one Chinese – and turned itself into an island to save them.

Boats to Kusu, for the time being, leave from Marina South Pier (Map pp52–3, H3) at 10am and 2pm Monday to Friday; 9am, noon and 3pm Saturday; 9am, 11am, 1pm, 3pm and 5pm Sunday.

across white-hot coals to demonstrate faith. Place to be: Sri Mariamman Temple (p51).

Singapore Buskers' Festival

It all feels a little forced, but this showcase of street-performing talent succeeds in injecting colour and life into Singapore's streets. Places to be: Orchard Rd and the Quays.

DECEMBER

Christmas

Celebrated with a predictable consumerist frenzy, which, as elsewhere, seems to start several months beforehand. Singapore's

Christmas is notable for the breathtaking light display (and not so breathtaking displays of giant Santas, house-sized presents and suchlike) that stretches the entire length of Orchard Rd. The light-up ceremony is in mid-November.

Hari Raya Haji

An event celebrating the conclusion of the pilgrimage to Mecca. Animals (mostly sheep) are ritually slaughtered in the mosques, after which the *Koran* dictates a portion of the meat must be handed out to the poor. The event will take place in November in 2010 and 2011.

The view of Singapore's soaring CBD skyline from Cavenagh Bridge

ITINERARIES

Singapore, unlike many cities, doesn't impose geographic restrictions on your day; it's just 40 minutes in a taxi between opposite corners of the island. It's perfectly feasible to spend a morning on Sentosa and an afternoon on Pulau Ubin. And despite the energy-sapping climate, you're usually never too far from a refreshing breeze or blissful dose of air-conditioning.

DAY ONE

Start with a stroll through the Singapore Botanic Gardens (p117), followed by eats and coffee at Halia (p123). Catch a bus to Orchard Rd and spend a few hours in retail heaven – or hell (see the boxed text, p42). Have lunch at Food Republic (p44), pick up some treats at the Takashimaya basement, then head for the National Museum of Singapore (p70). Afterwards, take the back exit, walk through Fort Canning Park (p39), then past Parliament to the Asian Civilisations Museum (p67). Have dinner by the bay at the Pierside Kitchen & Bar (p75), then either stroll to the Swissôtel, the Stamford and up 70 floors for quiet drinks at City Space (p76), or head for the noisier nightlife of Clarke Quay for a dance at Cuba Libre (p76).

DAY TWO

Take the MRT to Little India (p82) and spend the morning shopping and temple-spotting. Stop for lunch at Tekka Centre (p93), then take a cab to the Singapore Zoo (p48) for the afternoon. If you don't feel like staying for the Night Safari (p48), go back to Raffles Hotel in town for a few tipples at the Bar & Billiard Room (p76), then cab it up to Arab St for a Middle Eastern feast and a *shisha* (flavoured tobacco smoked in a hookah), followed by drinks at BluJaz Café (p93).

DAY THREE

Begin the day in the leafy heights of Mt Faber Park (p135), before taking the monorail across to Sentosa Island. Take a Segway tour of the island (p103), or, if speed is more your thing, have a few runs on the Sentosa Luge (p103). Find a spot for a laze on the beach then have lunch at Coastes (p100). Walk down the beach to Fort Siloso (p98), visit

---

Top left Singapore's mega entertainment complex, St James Power Station (p134) **Top right** Families will enjoy riding on the Skyride (p103) on Sentosa **Bottom** Escape from the hustle-bustle with a walk in the Singapore Botanic Gardens (p117)

Underwater World (p99) if it's not too crowded then take in the Songs of the Sea (p99) show. Afterwards, nip across the bridge to Keppel Island for drinks and dinner by the water at Privé (134), followed by a night out at the St James Power Station (p134).

DAY FOUR

You got bumped off your flight, so head for the Singapore Flyer (p73) for a quick spin. Then go to Changi Village and take a bumboat across to Pulau Ubin (p114) to spend the day cycling through the jungle followed by a stroll along the boardwalk at Tanjong Chek Jawa. Afterwards head back to the 'mainland' and go to East Coast Park (Map p105, F3) to relax on the beach. Finish off with seafront curry at the Mango Tree (p108).

Giraffes at Singapore Zoo (p48)

FORWARD PLANNING

Three weeks before you go Visit some of the Singapore websites (p192) and check out the Singapore Tourism Board online calendar for upcoming events. Book a table at Au Jardin Les Amis (p123) or, if you prefer a Chinese feast, book at My Humble House (p75). Check to see if your visit coincides with any holidays or festivals (p23) – you might want your hotel to be close to (or far from) a celebration.

One week before you go Check for concerts at the Esplanade (p67) and book tickets. Check with BluJaz Café (p93) for the following week's concerts. Read the *Straits Times'* Stomp website (www.stomp.com.sg) to get an idea of the day-to-day issues (just don't expect any political discussion).

One day before you go Check the Singapore Tourism calendar for last-minute updates. Buy Singapore dollars. Phone the catsitter. Check the newspapers to make sure the government hasn't been overthrown in a coup.

RAINY DAY

Singapore is known for scorching sunshine and sudden, heavy downpours, so the city is designed for shelter. If it's pouring, head for the museums (p170), or explore the underground warren of shops inside the City Link Mall (Map pp68–9, F4) – it's possible to spend half a day down there without ever poking your head above ground.

FOR FREE

Singapore Inc is not fond of offering its products for nothing, but there are ways to enjoy yourself, even if you've just lost your wallet. The Buddha Tooth Relic Temple & Museum (p51) is free to enter – and there's free vegetarian food in the basement. After that, a stroll through Fort Canning Park (p39) or Kent Ridge Park (p129) is a pleasant way to fill a couple of hours. If it's lunchtime, the Singapore Art Museum (p71) has free entry between noon and 2pm on weekdays, and from 6pm to 9pm Friday. The Esplanade (p67) also stages regular free Friday concerts and there are sometimes free classical concerts in the Singapore Botanic Gardens (p117). If evening is creeping close, next to Fort Canning Park is the National Museum of Singapore (p70), where the excellent Living Galleries are free between 6pm and 9pm.

The imposing gothic gate at Fort Canning Park (p39) was built in 1846

Girls preparing to perform an Indian dance

NEIGHBOURHOODS

The compact layout of Singapore's city centre and its excellent public-transport system make scooting between neighbourhoods easy, despite the wilting heat and occasional spectacular downpours. Even if you're walking, the city's abundant greenery often provides plenty of shade.

The ethnic enclaves Sir Stamford Raffles created with his original town plan resulted in sharply delineated districts that still exist in some form today. At the heart of it all is the Colonial District, hugging the mouth and the north bank of the Singapore River and brimming with elegant Victorian-era buildings, many of which (such as Raffles Hotel) are icons of the city.

Spreading along the river are the thriving quays, home to countless waterside restaurants, pubs, bars and clubs, while west of the district, the Doric columns suddenly give way to the brash, towering edifices that line Orchard Rd, Singapore's famous shopping strip.

Head north from the Colonial District and the transformation is equally dramatic, as the sugar-white facade of the Raffles Hotel recedes and bustling Bugis St Market passes by, the faces on the streets change and there is Little India, minutes away but a world apart. South of the river, beyond the dramatic thicket of CBD skyscrapers, lies Chinatown, home to both the tackiest side of the tourist trade and some of the coolest nightlife.

Leave the city heading east and things change again as the traditional Malay and Straits Chinese (Peranakan) districts of Geylang and Katong emerge, with streets lined with old tatty shophouses and dens of vice in Geylang, and the more decorous, dignified eating houses and restored buildings of Katong. Laid along the fringe of these two areas is the long ribbon of East Coast Park.

West of the city, past the sublime Botanic Gardens, are the affluent condominiums and landed properties of Holland Rd and Bukit Timah, hiding pockets of offbeat shops and fancy restaurants.

And lying off the coast to the south is Sentosa, Singapore's reborn fantasy island.

Eastern
Singapore
(p105)

Katong

Geylang
Serai

Geylang

Kallang

Strait of
Singapore

Little India &
the Arab Quarter
(p84-5)

Colonial
District
& the Quays
(pp68-9)

Marina
Bay

Marina
South

Orchard Rd
(pp40-1)

Chinatown
& the CBD
(pp2-3)

Keppel
Harbour

Selat Sengkir

Holland Rd &
Bukit Timah
(pp118-19)

Queenstown

Southwest
Singapore
(pp130-1)

Sentosa
Island
(p97)

To Jurong
(p137)

Pasir
Panjang

N

0   2 miles

0   4 km

>ORCHARD ROAD

A veritable canyon of concrete, glass and steel, Orchard Rd is a monument to the Singaporean obsession with shopping, though it's really a chicken-and-egg proposition: did the obsession spawn the malls, or did the malls spawn the obsession?

Either way, Singaporeans love these monoliths, spending vast amounts of leisure time bathing in icy air-conditioning, shopping, eating, drinking and movie-going.

Orchard Rd is the Mecca for this retail religion. While a certain sameness has begun to creep into many malls – chain stores and restaurants colonise space, and high rents push out the small-timers – many shops, particularly the older ones, retain their ability to surprise.

It's not all shallow commercialism either. At the eastern end of Orchard Rd are the hugely impressive National Museum of Singapore, Singapore Art Museum and the Peranakan Museum, and looming over them is the blissful oasis of Fort Canning Park.

ORCHARD ROAD

◉ SEE
Fort Canning Park **1** H6
The Battle Box..............(see 1)

🛍 SHOP
Apple Centre ....(see 17)
Cathay Cineleisure
  Orchard **2** F4
Centrepoint **3** G4
Far East Plaza **4** F3
Far East Shopping
  Centre **5** E4
Forum – The Shopping
  Mall **6** E3
Heeren **7** G4
HMV...............................(see 7)
Ion Orchard Mall **8** E4
Kinokuniya ....(see 9)
Louis Vuitton ....(see 9)
m)phosis ....(see 9)

Ngee Ann City **9** F4
Orchard Central **10** G5
Palais Renaissance **11** E3
Paragon **12** F4
Plaza Singapura **13** H5
Supernature **14** D4
Tanglin Mall **15** D4
Tanglin Shopping
  Centre **16** D3
Toys 'R' Us ....(see 6)
Wheelock Place **17** E4
Wisma Atria Shopping
  Centre **18** F4

🍴 EAT
Bombay Woodlands
  Restaurant ....(see 16)
Din Tai Fung ....(see 12)
Food Republic ....(see 18)
Marmalade Pantry .... (see 11)

Newton Circus **19** G2
Nuoc **20** G5
Projectshop Café
  Scene ....(see 12)
Shang Palace **21** D3

🍸 DRINK
Dubliners **22** G5
Ice Cold Beer **23** G4
Muddy Murphy's **24** E3
No 5 ....**25** G4
Orchard Towers **26** E3
Que Pasa **27** G4

⭐ PLAY
National Youth Centre
  Skate Park **28** F5

Please see over for map

👁 SEE

👁 FORT CANNING PARK

Once you get over the climb up the stairs, Fort Canning is not only a wonderful hilltop retreat from the city filled with shady paths and hidden nooks, it's a fascinating historical site. Check out the huge fort doors, the former barracks building, the spice garden and the Battle Box museum.

👁 THE BATTLE BOX

☎ 6333 0510; www.legendsfortcanning /fortcanning/battlebox.htm; 51 Canning Rise; adult/child $8/5; 🕙 10am-6pm; Ⓜ Dhoby Ghaut

Site of the former headquarters of the British Malaya Command, now a museum recreating the last hours before the fall of Singapore to the Japanese on 15 February, 1942, using reasonably lifelike

BAG LADIES

Salivating handbag fetishists can send themselves to leather heaven on level 3 of the **DFS Galleria** and at **Paragon**: Louis Vuitton, Fendi, Gucci, Salvatore Ferragamo, Burberry, Dior, Prada, Coach, Valentino, YSL and Loewe! Bag yourself a bargain, or beat your credit card into submission. The less brand-conscious might try Far East Plaza (p43), BHG at Parco Bugis Junction (p89) or hunt down knock-offs at the Bugis St Market (p87).

GETTING THERE & AROUND

> **MRT** – Orchard, Somerset and Dhoby Ghaut stations run west to east.
> **Bus** – 36, 124, 162, 174 and 518 run the length of the road.

wax figures and unsettling audio effects simulating the bombing.

🛍 SHOP

🛍 ION ORCHARD MALL *Mall*

☎ 6835 8748; www.ionorchard.com; 2 Orchard Turn; 10am-10pm; Ⓜ Orchard The most striking mall on Orchard, this futuristic, curvaceous glass-and-steel shrine to consumerism is bound to become one of the most photographed structures in Singapore. Dozens of high-end boutiques (any one of which could max out your credit card) and a basement food court to die for!

🛍 KINOKUNIYA *Bookshop*

☎ 6737 5021; 03-09/15, Ngee Ann City, 391 Orchard Rd; 🕙 10am-9pm; Ⓜ Orchard, Somerset; ♿
As vast as it is magnificent, entering Southeast Asia's largest bookshop is a trek into a literary jungle from which you might never emerge. One day they'll find a 40-year-old behind the Pets section who wandered in here when he was 12.

See Little India & Arab Quarter
Map pp84-5

E | F | G | H

1

Eew Boon Rd

Keng Chin Rd

Newton Rd

Surrey Rd

Lincoln Rd

Dunearn Rd

2

Balmoral Rd

Balmoral Park

Goodwood Hill

Surtee Rd

Keng Lee Rd

Kampong Java Rd

Hooper Rd

Kampong Java Park

Stevens Rd

Newton M

Bukit Timah Rd

Monk's Hill Tce

Scotts Rd

Clemenceau Ave Nth

Draycott Park

Anthony Rd

Peck Hay Rd

3

Draycott Rd

Draycott Dr

Draycott Hill

Mt Elizabeth Hospital

Cairnhill Rd

Mount Elizabeth Rd

Lavender Rd

Istana Park

24 Orchard Towers
20
11

Claymore Rd

Royal Thai Embassy

Paterson Rd

Ramsay Rd

German Embassy

Singapore Marriott

Qantas

Emerald Hill Rd

Central Expy

4

17

8 Orchard

Singapore Airlines

18

Orchard Rd

Bideford Rd

12

Hullet Rd

23
27
25

3

Edinburgh Rd

Orchard Turn

9 Orchard Post Office

Orchard Blvd

Orchard Link

7

Singapore Visitors Centre @ Orchard

13

Jl Tupai

Jl Arnap

Paterson Hill

28

Grange Rd

Somerset M

Penang Rd

10 20

Grange Rd

PUB Building

22

Dhoby Ghaut M

Indian High Commission

Devonshire Rd

Exeter Rd

Eber Rd

Oxley Rd

Clemenceau Ave

5

Ministry of Education Teachers' Network

Irwell Bank

Hoot Kiam Rd

Leonie Hill

Leonie Hill Rd

St Thomas Walk

St Thomas Wk

Killiney Rd

Comcentre Post Centre

Lloyd Rd

Oxley Rise

Oxley Wk

LOVE Sculpture

Zion Rd

Kim Seng Rd

River Valley Rd

Kim Yam Rd

Oxley Rd

Tank Rd

Fort Canning Park

1

6

Great World City

Occupational Safety & Health Centre

See Colonial District &
the Quays
Map pp68-9

🏠 LOUIS VUITTON *Fashion*
☎ 6734 7760; 01-07, Ngee Ann City, 391 Orchard Rd; 🕙 10.30am-9pm; Ⓜ Orchard, Somerset; ♿

It's worth going at weekends just to see the queues of eager females and their anxious male companions waiting to get in.

ORCHARD MALL CRAWL

Singapore's shopping malls embody the prosperity and abundance so deeply craved by its citizens. The major malls open their doors around 10am and stay open until the last movie-goers and food court—feasters go home around midnight. The following are the major malls, heading roughly from east to west:

> **Tanglin Mall** (Map pp40-1; 163 Tanglin Rd) Expat haven (check the crowds of wives at Caffé Beviamo) with an excellent gourmet supermarket, shops for mothers and midrange boutiques.

> **Tanglin Shopping Centre** (Map pp40-1; 19 Tanglin Rd) The place for art, antiques and carpets. Try **Antiques of the Orient** (02-40) for maps, charts and photos, or the Asian academic titles at **Select Books** (03-15).

> **Wheelock Place** (Map pp40-1; 501 Orchard Rd) Apple devotees make pilgrimage to the mall's glass cone, which also houses a packed Borders and exclusive hair salons.

> **Ion Orchard Mall** (p39) Any mall that actually alters the flow of pedestrian traffic is a pretty big deal. If the roster of tenants – including Armani, Dior and Cartier – is anything to go by, the Ion is destined to be among Singapore's classiest.

> **Wisma Atria** (Map pp40-1; 435 Orchard Rd) In-your-face frontage contains international high-street fashion, jewellery and electronics, and outstanding Food Republic food court.

> **Ngee Ann City** (Map pp40-1; 391 Orchard Rd) Chocolate blancmange—coloured doyen of Orchard, with Takashimaya department store (with fabulous basement food centre), the vast Kinokuniya bookshop, and resident gods Cartier, Chanel and Louis Vuitton.

> **Paragon** (Map pp40-1; 290 Orchard Rd) Classy, classy, classy: Givenchy, Ralph Lauren, YSL, Hugo Boss, Versace, Gucci, Jean-Paul Gaultier, Prada and people who love them. Great basement food selection.

> **Cathay Cineleisure Orchard** (Map pp40-1; 8 Grange Rd) Specialising in teen fashion and junk food, with a cinema and possibly the worst escalator layout on earth.

> **Centrepoint** (Map pp40-1; 176 Orchard Rd) Lively mall housing flagship old-world Robinson's department store (great staff).

> **Plaza Singapura** (Map pp40-1; 68 Orchard Rd) Vast even by Orchard Rd standards and home to a 10-screen cinema, Carrefour supermarket, homeware, Barang Barang Asian furniture, fashion, food...everything!

> **The Cathay** (Map pp68-9; 2 Handy Rd) Streetwear, beauty and nail salons, 'lifestyle' shops and the excellent Picturehouse cinema behind an unfinished-looking Art Deco frontage.

KIDS 'R' US

Singapore's kids and teens are commercially catered for by a gaggle of clothes and toy shops. Here are some of the best places for kids and teens:

> **Bugis St Market** Two levels of cheap street clothes, bags, shoes and manicurists; see p87.
> **Far East Plaza** (Map pp40-1; 14 Scotts Rd) Teen mall most popular for cheap streetwear. Also hair and beauty salons, tattoo parlours, jewellery, electronics and secondhand books. Haggling possible.
> **Forum – The Shopping Mall** (Map pp40-1; 583 Orchard Rd; 10am-10pm) Kid-sized DKNY, Ralph Lauren, Guess and Benetton gear.
> **Heeren** (Map pp40-1; 260 Orchard Rd) Hip, youth-orientated monolith, with massive multilevel HMV and warrens of local designer outlets on levels 4 and 5.
> **Kinokuniya** Kids' books by the truckload; see p39.
> **Mothercare** (Map pp68-9; ☎ 6513 3212; 02-03, Suntec City; 11.30am-9pm) For all your bootie and mollycoddling requirements.
> **Robinsons** (Map pp68-9; ☎ 6733 0888; Centrepoint, 176 Orchard Rd; 10.30am-10pm) A family-focused department store.
> **Toys 'R' Us** (Map pp40-1; ☎ 6235 4322; 03-03/25 Forum Shopping Mall, 583 Orchard Rd; 10am-10pm) A celebration of international toydom.

Join the queue, and look for a bag the replica hounds haven't copied yet.

M)PHOSIS Fashion
☎ 6737 6539; B1-09/10, Ngee Ann City, 391 Orchard Rd; 10.30am-9.30pm; M Orchard, Somerset;

M)phosis' Ngee Ann City branch (one of nine around town) stocks colour-coded miniature wisps of girly, slinky, sexy stuff; nice knits; and elegant pieces by local designer Colin Koh. You'll probably increase your chances of actually fitting into something if you buy two pieces and sew them together.

SUPERNATURE Food
☎ 6304 1336; Park House, 21 Orchard Blvd; 10am-7pm Mon-Sat, 10am-6pm Sun; M Orchard

Supernature is Singapore's best organic deli. Its shelves are heaving with chemical- and gluten-free vegies, groceries, baby food, wine and meats. There's a juice bar in the main shop, and vitamins and supplements are sold in the annex next door.

THAT CD SHOP Music
☎ 6238 6720; 01-01/02, Pacific Plaza, 9 Scotts Rd; 11am-midnight; M Orchard

Filling a two-storey warehouse with stacks of CDs, comfy leather

THAI'D TO TRADITION

With new shopping malls being shoe-horned into every available space on Orchard Rd, why, many visitors ask, does the Thai Embassy occupy such large, prominent grounds in an area of staggeringly expensive real estate? Back in the 1990s, the Thai government was reportedly offered $139 million for the site, but they turned it down. Why? Because selling the land, bought by Thailand for $9000 in 1893 by the revered King Chulalongkorn (Rama V), would be seen as an affront to his memory. And so, happily, it remains, drooled over by frustrated developers.

couches, subtle downlights, free coffee and a Nakamichi sound system that sets the chandeliers a-rockin', this feels less like consumerism and more like a party. Consider moving in on a permanent basis.

🍴 EAT
🍴 BOMBAY WOODLANDS
Indian, Vegetarian $$
☎ 6836 6961; B1-12, Tanglin Shopping Centre, 19 Tanglin Rd; ⏱ 11am-3pm & 6-10pm; Ⓜ Orchard; Ⓥ ♿
Moved from its original location to a new spot a few doors down, this is still one of the hidden gems of the Orchard area. Try the bottomless lunchtime buffet or choose

from the small but uniformly excellent menu of vegetarian staples.

🍴 DIN TAI FUNG *Taiwanese* $$
☎ 6836 8336; B1-03/06, Paragon Shopping Centre, 290 Orchard Rd; ⏱ 11.30am-9.30pm Mon-Fri, 10am-10pm Sat & Sun; Ⓜ Orchard; ♿
Taiwanese restaurant acknowledged even by hype-resistant luminaries such as Anthony Bourdain as producing the best dumplings on Earth (though some insist that only applies to the Taiwanese original). The signature dumplings *(xiao long bao)* are nevertheless sublime, the beef noodle soup rich and hearty, and the shrimp-pork wanton soup delectable. Be prepared to queue, especially at weekends, but the wait is worth it. A must.

🍴 FOOD REPUBLIC
Food Court $
Level 4, Wisma Atria Shopping Centre, 435 Orchard Rd; ⏱ 11am-10.30pm; ♿ Ⓥ ♿
Perennially packed, it's survival of the quickest when it comes to grabbing a table at peak times, but the food is worth it. If it's full, head for the private sitting areas attached to the Chutneys Indian and Waan Waan Thai stalls, where you pay a little more. We also particularly like the teppanyaki counter and the beef noodles.

Sumithra Debi
Tattoo Artist

So much of your work is based on colour. Where do you go to experience bursts of colour in Singapore? I take a trip to the Botanic Gardens (p117) or go for a good long hike around Bukit Timah Nature Reserve (p117). **Good place to people watch?** Right here in Orchard Rd. Sit yourself in any of the long stone seats along Orchard Rd in front of Paragon (p42), Takashimaya (p42) or the Ion Mall (p39), get yourself an ice cream for a dollar and watch the fashionable people go by. **Any good places for girls with curves to clothes shop?** Holland Village (p122) has a number of smaller dress shops that have been known as the place where expat women go to find their sizes and tastes. **Best view of Singapore at night?** On top of Mt Faber. There is also a place called the Jewel Box (p133) that has a number of beautiful chill-out spots.

🍴 MARMALADE PANTRY

Cafe $$

☎ 6734 2700; B1-08, Palais Renaissance, 390 Orchard Rd; ⏰ 10am-10pm; Ⓜ Orchard; ♿ Ⓥ 🚻

Crisp white tablecloths, comfy booths and affluent ladies sizing each other up over the glossy mags set the scene at this sub-street cafe serving tasty morsels. The place to be seen on Sunday mornings, if you're not at a brunch (see boxed text, p77).

🍴 NEWTON CIRCUS

Hawker Centre $

Scotts Rd; ⏰ 5pm-4am; Ⓜ Newton; ♿ Ⓥ 🚻

Vibrant and noisy, this famous hawker centre still has a great atmosphere. You could eat here for a whole year and never get bored. Well-known stalls include Boon Tat BBQ seafood, Hup Kee oyster omelette (stall 65) and, next to it, Singapore's most famous fishball noodles. Touts can be a problem for foreigners, but ignore them. The best stalls don't need to tout.

🍴 NUOC *Vietnamese* $$

☎ 6884 6808; www.nuoc.com.sg; 12-01, Orchard Central, 181 Orchard Rd; ⏰ noon-3pm & 6-10pm Mon-Fri, noon-10pm Sat & Sun; Ⓜ Sommerset; Ⓥ

High-end Vietnamese cuisine is served with a spectacular view

at this restaurant on the roof of the Orchard Central mall. Traditional dishes such as stir-fried lemongrass and ginger chicken and clay-pot soups are excellent choices, but the house special is a romantic Vietnamese hot pot for two.

🍴 PROJECTSHOP CAFÉ

International $$

☎ 6735 6765; 02-20/21, Paragon Shopping Centre, 290 Orchard Rd; ⏰ 9.30am-10.30pm; Ⓜ Orchard; ♿ Ⓥ 🚻

Sit out in the mall to watch Singapore's affluent sashay past, or sit inside the shop linked to the cafe for a more private setting. Sandwiches and pastas are reasonable, but the real reason to come here is the stupendous desserts. Banana Cream Pie tops our list, or try the key lime pie if you need a serious sugar hit.

🍴 SHANG PALACE

Chinese $$$

☎ 6213 4473; Ground, Shangri-La Hotel, 22 Orange Grove Rd; ⏰ 11.30am-2.30pm & 6.30-10.30pm Mon-Fri, 10.30am-2.30pm & 6.30-10.30pm Sat & Sun; Ⓜ Orchard, then taxi; ♿

Among the best of the city's Chinese restaurants, Shang's sumptuous interior is matched by its Cantonese food. Seafood is a particular speciality, along with classics such as Peking Duck, and there's a *dim sum* menu, if you

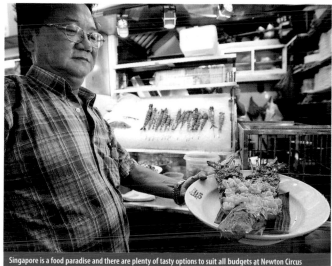

Singapore is a food paradise and there are plenty of tasty options to suit all budgets at Newton Circus

want the atmosphere without the expense. Book in advance at weekends.

DRINK

DUBLINERS *Irish Pub*
☎ 6735 2200; 165 Penang Rd;
⏲ 11.30am-1am Sun-Thu, till 2am Fri & Sat; Ⓜ Somerset
Lousy Irish pubs filled with bellowing, beer-bellied execs are omnipresent in Singapore. However, this white colonial heritage building is a cut above the rest. Choose between the rough

floorboards and cosy gloom inside, and nursing a Guinness and braving the traffic noise on the verandah.

MUDDY MURPHY'S *Irish Pub*
☎ 6735 0400; Orchard Hotel Shopping Arcade; ⏲ 11.30am-1am Mon-Thu, till 2am Fri & Sat, till midnight Sun
OK, OK, it's another Irish pub, but the substreet-level courtyard also singles this one out from the rest and makes it a perfect retreat from Orchard Rd. Live bands play here regularly – a few of the deedly-dee variety.

WORTH THE TRIP

The **Singapore Zoo and Night Safari** (☎ 6269 3411; www.zoo.com.sg, www.nightsafari .com.sg; 80 Mandai Lake Rd; zoo only adult/child $18/12, zoo tram $5/3, Night Safari $22/15, combined zoo/Night Safari $32/20, children on birthday free; 🕑 zoo 8.30am-6pm, Night Safari 7.30pm-midnight; Ⓜ Ang Mo Kio, then bus 138; ♿) are both world-class, with the zoo being constantly upgraded.

The zoo's showpiece animals include endangered white rhinos, Bengal white tigers, polar bears, baboons and orang-utans. Wherever possible, moats replace bars, and the zoo is beautifully spread out over 28 hectares of lush greenery beside the Upper Seletar Reservoir.

Highlights are many – from the moment you step in to be greeted by free-ranging cotton-top tamarins and white-faced sakis and siamangs cavorting in the trees. The baboon enclosure, a large sandy area with cliffs, a waterfall and a stream fashioned to look like the Ethiopian hinterland, is worth the entrance fee alone.

Other primate areas also allow you to watch the likes of gibbons, the lively capuchins or proboscis monkeys, while the orang-utans, once marooned on a small island surrounded by gawping humans, have been cut loose and now get to hang around in the trees gawping down on the humans instead.

Another favourite is the Fragile Forest, a large netted dome where you'll have lemurs trotting across your path, flying foxes dangling by your head and hundreds of butterflies fluttering past your face.

Feeding times are staggered to allow you to catch most of them as you walk around, and the Zoo's tours (check the website) are worth joining.

Some shows, such as those at the Elephants of Asia and polar-bear enclosures, may be a little circus-like for some – and there has been particular controversy surrounding the keeping of polar bears in a hot equatorial climate.

Next door, but completely separate from the zoo, is the acclaimed Night Safari. This 40-hectare forested park is home to 120 different species of animals, including tigers, lions and leopards. In the darkness the moats and other barriers seem to melt away and it actually looks like these creatures could walk over and take a bite out of you. The atmosphere is heightened even further by the herds of strolling antelope, which often pass within inches of the electric trams that take you around.

For an even creepier experience, walk through the enclosed Mangrove Walk, where bats flap around your head and dangle from trees a few feet above your head.

Visitors looking to do both parks in one trip can chill over dinner and drinks in the food court between the zoo's closing and the Night Safari's opening.

If returning from the Night Safari by bus, you should aim to be on the bus by around 10.45pm to ensure you make the last train leaving Ang Mo Kio MRT at 11.28pm. A taxi to or from the city centre at that time costs around $20; there is a taxi stand outside, but the queues are often long and cabs can be maddeningly infrequent.

EMERALD HILL

A cobbled pedestrianised lane of crumbling, lantern-lit shophouses – there can be few more atmospheric spots in the city to stop for a drink. That is until you realise it's all a bit of a charade. That little neighbourhood strip of bars is entirely owned by a single company. But despite this, the drinking holes are all good, drawing crowds of locals and tourists alike.

The best are the Asian retro **No 5** (☎ 6732 0818; noon-2am Mon-Thu, noon-3am Sat, 5pm-2am Sun), Mediterranean-style wine-and-tapas bar **Que Pasa** (☎ 6235 6626; 1.30pm-2am Mon-Thu, 1.30pm-3am Fri & Sat, 5.30pm-2am Sun) and raucous rock pub **Ice Cold Beer** (☎ 6735 9929; 5pm-2am Sun-Thu, 5pm-3am Fri & Sat).

☿ ORCHARD TOWERS
Bars & Clubs
400 Orchard Rd; Ⓜ Orchard
Known locally as 'four floors of whores', the Orchard Towers are home to massage parlours and a couple of pick-up bars, most

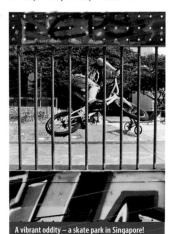
A vibrant oddity – a skate park in Singapore!

notably the **Ipanema World Music Bar** (☎ 6738 3483; 2nd fl; 7pm-5am Mon-Thu, 7pm-6am Fri & Sat, 1pm-4am Sun). However, there's also the sports-friendly Aussie pub **Downunder** (☎ 6238 8419; 3rd fl; 11am-2am). Out back is where you'll find **3-Monkeys** (☎ 6735 3707; 11am-5am), home of local transvestite comedy legend Kumar.

★ PLAY

☆ NATIONAL YOUTH CENTRE SKATE PARK *Skate Park*
☎ 6309 0046; Penang Rd; 7am-11pm; Ⓜ Somerset; ♿
One of Singapore's better attempts at embracing modern youth culture, the National Youth Centre Skate Park is fully equipped with ramps and rails where boarders and bikers practise, pose and impress watching members of the opposite sex. Occasionally, a temporary stage is set up for concerts.

>CHINATOWN & THE CBD

Just in time, Singapore realised Chinatown's narrow lanes of old shop-houses, with their shuttered windows and steep tiled roofs, were fit for more than tearing down. This old district, once home to opium dens, death houses, brothels and gang warfare, is still Singapore's most colourful.

Even within Chinatown there are distinct ethnic centres: Hokkien on Havelock Rd and Telok Ayer, China and Chulia Sts; Teochew on Circular Rd, Boat Quay and Upper South Bridge Rd; Cantonese on Lower South Bridge and New Bridge Rds and Upper Cross St.

Pagoda, Temple and Trengganu Sts are the centre of the tatty tourist trade but have some decent antique shops. Market-weary visitors also head for the Sri Mariamman and Buddha Tooth Relic temples. Cross South Bridge Rd into a different world of top restaurants, hip bars, boutiques and trendy businesses packed into narrow Club St and Ann Siang Rd.

A stroll over Ann Siang Hill Park leads to Amoy and Telok Ayer Sts, a historical district of temples and shophouse eateries. Surrounding it all to the east and north are the looming skyscrapers of Singapore's financial district.

CHINATOWN & THE CBD

◉ SEE

🏠 SHOP

🍴 EAT

🍸 DRINK

🌟 PLAY

Please see over for map

⊙ SEE

⊙ BUDDHA TOOTH RELIC TEMPLE & MUSEUM

☎ 6220 0220; www.btrts.org.sg;
288 South Bridge Rd; admission free;
⌚ 7am-7pm, relic viewing from
8am-6pm; Ⓜ Chinatown; ♿

Impressive temple and museum constructed in 2007 primarily to house a Buddha Tooth Relic, which sits inside a 420kg solid-gold stupa in a dazzlingly ornate 4th-floor room. Get there at 10.30am or 7.30pm, when monks hold ceremonies to open the chamber. Also worth seeing are the peaceful rooftop garden, where a huge prayer wheel sits inside a 10,000 Buddha Pavilion, and the museum and the 100 Dragons Hall. Donations for upkeep of the temple and relic are welcome.

⊙ CHINATOWN HERITAGE CENTRE

☎ 6221 9556; www.chinatownheritage
centre.sg; 48 Pagoda St; adult/child $10/6;
⌚ 9am-6.30pm; Ⓜ Chinatown; ♿

One of Singapore's less-trumpeted museums, this is one of our favourites: an evocative exploration of the grim, tough lives of early Chinese immigrants. Particularly effective are re-creations of the living conditions people in the area endured. There's a lot to take in, so keep your ticket stub and you can step out for a breather and return later.

⊙ SRI MARIAMMAN TEMPLE

☎ 6223 4064; 244 South Bridge Rd;
⌚ 7am-noon, 6-9pm;
Ⓜ Chinatown; ♿

The colourful *gopuram* (entrance tower) of Singapore's oldest Hindu temple, built in its present form in 1843, with dozens of additions since, is one of the most photographed objects in the city. Sadly,

Sri Mariamman Temple in all its colourful glory

See Colonial District & the Quays Map pp68-9

E

F

G

H

Read St

Coleman Bridge

Clarke Quay

Riverwalk Galleria

Elgin Bridge

The Padang

1

Merchant Rd

Eu Tong Sen St

New Bridge Rd

Hill St

Carpenter St

Hongkong St

N Canal Rd

Empress Pl

Esplanade Park

Esplanade Bridge

Anderson Bndge

Esplanade Dr

Singapore River

Cavanagh Bridge

Merlion

South Bridge Rd

Circular Rd

First Generation Sculpture

5

Hong Lim Park

Kucinta Sculpture

Fullerton Rd

One Fullerton

2

Upper Pickering St

Reclining Figures Sculpture

Bird Sculpture

Chinatown Point

Upper Hokien St

Pidemco Centre

George St

Homage to Newton Sculpture

Chula St

Bonham St

Battery Rd

Church St

25

OCBC Centre

UOB Plaza

Collyer Quay

Hong Lim Complex

Hoklen St

Phillip St

Market St

Raffles Place

Cathay Pacific Airways

Singapore Motor Launch Owners Association

11

Nankin St

China St

Malacca St

Ocean Building

Marina Bay

Mosque St

Chin Chew St

30

32

Far East Square

Republic Plaza

Air New Zealand

6

37

26

38

Telok Ayer St

China Sq Food Ct

Singapore International Chamber of Commerce

9

Club St

40

36

18

20

Cross St

Robinson Rd

8

33

14

23

29

Ann Siang Hill

Boon Tat St

Thai Airways

Erskine Rd

31

Telok Ayer Garden

Amoy St

7

Market St

16

Ann Siang Hill Park

Stanley St

Telok Ayer St

21

URA Centre

Cecil St

24

Robinson Rd

Maxwell Link

Katagasullur Rd

McCallum St

Raffles Quay

Maxwell Rd

Peck Seah St

UIC Building

0   200 m
0   0.1 miles

Marina South

Tanjong Pagar

Guan St

Marina Station Rd

International Plaza

Treasury Building

M

Prince Edward Rd

MAS Building

6

tourists crowd its magnificent door and its many shrines, outnumbering worshippers much of the time. Wait for a moment when there are no coach parties.

THIAN HOCK KENG TEMPLE
☎ 6423 4626; 158 Telok Ayer St;
🕐 7.30am-5.30pm; Ⓜ Chinatown, Tanjong Pagar, Raffles Place
Oddly, while Chinatown's most famous Hindu temple is swamped, its most famous Chinese temple is often a haven of tranquillity. It's

a beautiful, serene place, which was once a favourite landing point for Chinese sailors, before land reclamation pushed the sea far down the road.

🛍 SHOP
Though the main area of Chinatown has been swamped by stalls aimed at tourists (does anyone still buy those 'Fine City' T-shirts?), behind this wall of tattiness there are interesting antique, traditional-medicine and handicraft shops. Across South Bridge Rd, Club St has a few hip boutiques.

EU YAN SANG
Chinese Medicine
☎ 6223 5085; 269 South Bridge Rd;
🕐 9am-6pm; Ⓜ Chinatown; ♿
Venerable Eu Yan Sang has enjoyed the fruits of official efforts to propel traditional

FREEDOM OF SPEECH! (JUST DON'T MENTION FREEDOM OF SPEECH)
When Speakers' Corner (Map pp52–3) was established in Hong Lim Park in 2000, the ever spin-happy government and press hailed it as a step forward for Singaporean democracy and freedom of speech. Singaporeans love novelty, and in the first month 400 speakers addressed enthusiastic crowds. A year later only 11 braved the stand. Now, it's completely deserted and, cynics will say, a more accurate symbol of the state of free speech in a country that's politically apathetic anyway. In order to take your place at the soapbox, you have to be Singaporean, register in advance with local police, avoid blacklisted subjects such as religion, politics and ethnicity, and stay within Singapore's sedition laws. Still feel like speaking out?

REAPING THE PROFITS
Sharp-eyed wanderers will notice some curious objects on sale around Chinatown – miniature cars, houses, computers, mobile phones – all made of paper. They are offerings burned at funeral wakes to ensure the material needs of the dead are taken care of. Once, Sago Lane was home to so-called 'death houses', where people would place their dying relatives to spend their last days. This morbid practice was banned in 1961, but a few shops in the area, such as Nam's Supplies (Map pp52–3) on Smith St, still sell these paper objects.

Chinese medicine back into the mainstream, with modern clinics and branches overseas. You can consult a herbalist for $15, or get off-the-shelf remedies such as instant bird's nest (to tone the lung) or deer's tail pills (to invigorate the kidneys). Most remedies also come with English instructions.

FAR EAST LEGEND
Antiques, Handicrafts
☎ 6323 5365; 233 South Bridge Rd; 10.30am-6.30pm; Ⓜ Chinatown
Inside this homey, small and charmingly cluttered shop you'll find an excellent collection of furniture, lamps, handicrafts, statues and other *objets d'art* from all over Asia. Well worth exploring!

PEOPLE'S PARK COMPLEX
Chinese Souvenirs, Spas, Health Items
101 Upper Cross St; 10am-9.30pm; Ⓜ Chinatown
A great spot for Chinese souvenirs, gifts and shops specialising in health-related items. The real reason to come here is for the massage places that will vie for your patronage. Feeling adventurous? Try out one of the fish-pond foot spas on Level 3, where schools of fish nibble the dead skin right off your feet.

WANG SAN YANG *Teahouse*
☎ 6532 2707; www.wystm.com; Block 531, 01-61, Hong Lim Complex; 10am-9pm; Ⓜ Chinatown; ♿
Elegant speciality tea merchant whose location among the rough-and-ready bustle of the Hong Lim Complex gives it an injection of authenticity lacking in Chinatown's more tourist-friendly teahouses. Tea demonstrations on demand.

YUE HWA CHINESE PRODUCTS *Department Store*
☎ 6538 4222; 70 Eu Tong Sen St; 11am-9pm; Ⓜ Chinatown; ♿
This five-storey department store stocks everything Chinese, from porcelain teapots and jade jewellery to slinky silk cheongsams, dried fish and medicinal herbs,

fungi and spices. Pick up some ginseng, a snakeskin drum or a jar full of seahorses for the road.

🏠 ZHEN LACQUER GALLERY
Handicrafts

☎ 6222 2718; 1/1A/1B Trengganu St; 🕙 9.30am-6.30pm; Ⓜ Chinatown; ♿

Generally kitsch but sometimes stylish, the shiny lacquered stuff at Zhen will at least keep your eyes entertained for a few minutes. Hand-painted jewellery boxes, placemat sets, utensils, plates and photo albums are the pick of the crop.

🍴 EAT

The absence of malls makes Chinatown one of Singapore's best eating districts, where sweaty hawker centres and cheap coffee shops share pavement with world-class restaurants. Club St is the only exclusively upmarket area; everywhere else, the cheap and cheerful coexists happily with the rare and refined.

🍴 ANNALAKSHMI *Indian* $

☎ 6223 0809; www.annalakshmi .com.sg; 104 Amoy St; 🕙 11am-3pm

Erich's Wuerstelstand offers sausages and sauerkraut in Chinatown. Odd? Yes, but people love it.

Mon-Sat; Ⓜ Tanjong Pagar; ♿
Ⓥ ♨

Something of an institution, this volunteer-run Indian vegetarian restaurant serves up excellent limitless lunchtime buffets that attract hordes of office workers. When you're finished just pay whatever you feel like to the cashier. From $5 to $10 is acceptable – it all goes to charity. Other branches at Lau Pa Sat and in Chinatown Point are open for dinner as well.

🍴 BLUE GINGER *Peranakan* $$

☎ 6222 3928; 97 Tanjong Pagar Rd; ⏱ noon-2pm & 6-10pm; Ⓜ Tanjong Pagar; ♿ ♨

Fashionable, homely shophouse restaurant dishing up all the rich, spicy, sour Peranakan favourites, including the *ayam panggang* (grilled chicken in coconut and spices) that is the restaurant's claim to fame.

🍴 BREEZE *International* $$$

☎ 6511 3333; www.thescarlethotel. com; 31 Erskine Rd; ⏱ 6-10pm Mon-Thu, 6pm-midnight Fri & Sat, 5-11pm Sun; Ⓜ Tanjong Pagar, Chinatown; ♿ ♨

Slide into some designer togs and sashay up to the rooftop of the Scarlet Hotel with its impressive city views. Here the rich and fashionable dine on seafood feasts under the stars while keeping one eye on their phones.

🍴 BROTH *International* $$

☎ 6323 3353; www.broth.com.sg; 21 Duxton Hill; ⏱ noon-2.30pm & 6.30-10.30pm Mon-Thu, noon-2.30pm & 7-11pm Fri, 7pm-11pm Sat; Ⓜ Tanjong Pagar; ♿ Ⓥ

Set in a beautifully converted shophouse on a blissfully peaceful cobbled pedestrian street, Broth serves up excellent bistro classics (including a very good beef tenderloin). The signature dish (lamb loin in a green coat) is a must-try!

🍴 CI YAN ORGANIC VEGETARIAN HEALTH FOOD *Organic Vegetarian* $

☎ 6225 9026; 2 Smith St; noon-10pm; Ⓜ Chinatown; Ⓥ

Organic meals served 100% Buddhist style, meaning vegetarian, no garlic, onions or anything else that might disturb meditation. Wooden tables and chairs and spiritual books lend a holy atmosphere. Call first to hear a daily recording of what specials are on the menu.

🍴 ERICH'S WUERSTELSTAND *Austrian* $

☎ 9627 4882; Stall 2 & 3 Terrengganu St; ⏱ noon-11pm

An eccentric Austrian hawking very low priced sausages and sauerkraut from a stall in Chinatown – it's hardly a surprise this place

NEIGHBOURHOODS

CHINATOWN & THE CBD

Choices. Decisions. The Maxwell Rd Hawker Centre has more than 50 stalls under one roof

has achieved a certain fame. And deservedly so: what could be better than a hearty sausage and beer (from across the lane) after a hot day in the city? If the sausage is a bit too heavy for you, Erich also sells home-baked muffins, pastries and other less-wursty items.

🍴 HONG LIM COMPLEX
Hawker Centre　　　　　S

cnr South Bridge Rd & Upper Cross St; 🕙 **8am-10.30pm;** Ⓜ **Chinatown;** ♿
If you're sick of bumping elbows with tourists, head for this pocket of old-time Chinatown, where 'uncles' sit around watching the world go by and foreign faces still draw attention. The food centre is routinely crowded – try the famous **Outram Park Fried Kway Teow** (Block 531A, 02-18), or its rival, **Cuppage** (Block 536,

01-129). If the hawker centre looks too full or intimidating, try **Wuhan Food House** (01-33).

🍴 L'ANGELUS *French*　　$$$
☎ **6225 6897; 85 Club St;** 🕙 **noon-2pm Mon-Fri, 7pm-late Mon-Sat;** Ⓜ **Chinatown;** ♿
A cosy and unstuffy French bistro famed for its *escargot* and chocolate cake. If it's a rainy night, tuck into the warming, incredibly filling *cassoulet* (bean stew with meat and sausage) washed down with a glass of something red and robust.

🍴 LAU PA SAT FESTIVAL MARKET *Hawker Centre*　　S
18 Raffles Quay; 🕙 **some stalls 24hr;** Ⓜ **Raffles Place;** Ⓥ
Vying for the title of Most Famous Hawker Centre, this circular iron

structure dating back to 1894 even receives tour parties, who clamber from coaches and stand around looking uncomfortable. Singapore's 'upgrading' mania has bled some of the atmosphere from this venerable institution, but wandering its aisles and picking out your dinner is still a pleasure.

🍴 MAXWELL RD HAWKER CENTRE *Hawker Centre* $

cnr Maxwell Rd & South Bridge Rd;
🕑 7am-10pm; Ⓜ Tanjong Pagar;
Ⓖ Ⓥ

If you want to get down and local in Chinatown, Maxwell Rd is it (along with Chinatown Complex). Sip soupy, sump oil–like coffee with the 'uncles' in the morning, or battle the huge crowds at lunchtime. Stalls slip in and out of favour with Singapore's fickle diners so look for the queues to spot this week's fad. And who could pass up a bakery stall called Bread Pitt?

🍴 NANYANG OLD COFFEE
Coffee Shop $

☎ 6100 3450; 22/23 268 South Bridge Rd; 7.30am-8.30pm; 🚇 Chinatown; Ⓖ Ⓙ

If it's caffeine with character you crave, this traditional Singaporean coffee shop is a great spot to chill out and recharge with a frozen coffee drink after taking in the sights of the area. There's also a small 'Singapore Coffee Museum'

THE HAWKER CENTRE DECODED

It's not rocket science, but a visit to a hawker centre does require some insider knowledge.

> **First, find your table** Singaporeans always set up base camp before they go in search of food. And to do this, they use the humble packet of tissues. It confuses and confounds many newcomers, but to a Singaporean, a packet of tissues on a table or a seat is as good as erecting barbed wire and gun turrets – it means 'reserved'.

> **Second, find your food** Forget stall exclusivity – order as many things from as many stalls as you like, and ignore touts at places such as Newton Circus, East Coast Lagoon Food Village and Lau Pa Sat. It's actually illegal to tout.

> **Self-service, or delivery?** If a stall bears the sign 'self-service', that means you have to wait and carry the food to your table yourself. Other stalls ask where you're sitting and deliver food to you (which is why it's important to bag your table first).

> **Be seated and ye shall be found** Nearly all older hawker centres have roaming drinks staff, who will seek you out and take your order. At the more modern ones it's more usual to order from the drinks stalls.

> **Greasy hands?** Why do stalls never have tissues? Because most places are frequented by poverty-stricken tissue sellers, who'll come around selling five packets for a dollar. Help them out and buy some.

YOU AH, WHAT YOU EAT

A quick rundown of some classic Singapore dishes you're likely to encounter.

> **Ais Kacang** (Malay) Shaved ice covered with syrup, jelly, sweet corn and red beans.
> **Bak kut teh** (Hokkien) Pork-rib soup.
> **Bee hoon** (Hokkien) Thin rice-vermicelli noodles used in a variety of dishes.
> **Beef/chicken rendang** (Malay) Thick Malay-style curry.
> **Char kway teow** (Hokkien) Stir-fried noodles with cockles, Chinese sausage and egg in dark sauce.
> **Chicken rice** (Hainanese) Boiled chicken with stock-boiled rice and chilli-ginger dip.
> **Chilli crab** (Singaporean) Crab cooked with chilli, sweetish tomato sauce and egg.
> **Fish-head curry** (Indian) Single large fish head in spicy, rich, sour gravy, usually with tomato and okra.
> **Hokkien mee** (Hokkien) Yellow egg noodles stir-fried with prawns, pork and vegetables with an egg stirred in.
> **Katong laksa** (Malay) Rich, spicy coconut sauce with yellow or white noodles, prawns, cockles, fish cake, bean sprouts and laksa leaf.
> **Mee goreng** (Malay) Spicy fried noodles with tomato sauce, potato, cabbage and sometimes mutton.
> **Nasi lemak** (Malay) Coconut rice with fried fish and peanuts.
> **Oyster omelette** (Hokkien) Oysters fried with eggs, chives and tapioca flour.
> **Popiah** (Peranakan) Spring roll filled with vegetables and various meats or prawn.
> **Rojak** (Malay) Vegetable salad with chilli sauce, cucumber, fruit, onion and dough fritters.
> **Roti prata** (Indian) Fried flat bread (plain or with filling) served with curry sauce.
> **Sambal** (Malay) Condiment made from chilli, various spices and often shrimp paste, used to cook seafood, meat and vegetables.

in the back with cultural artefacts and historical relics – all coffee-related, of course.

🍴 OCEAN CURRY FISH HEAD
Chinese $

☎ 6324 9226; 181 Telok Ayer St; ⏱ 11am-8.30pm Mon-Fri, 11am-2am Sat; Ⓜ Tanjong Pagar; ♿ Specialising in a Chinese version of the infamous South Indian dish, this street-corner eatery

spills out onto the pavement at lunchtimes, when the plastic tables are full of office workers crowding around clay pots and mopping their foreheads. If the fish head doesn't appeal, try the prawn-paste chicken, fried squid or chilli *kang kong* (water spinach).

🍴 PEACH GARDEN *Chinese* $$
☎ 6535 7833; Level 33, OCBC Centre, 65 Chulia St; ⏱ 11.30am-2.30pm & 6-10pm; Ⓜ Raffles Place; ♿ Ⓥ

For a Chinese restaurant with a view, it's tough to beat this one. The food and service are immaculate too. Try to reserve a window table well in advance and tuck into superb dim sum, or try the duck, roast goose or lobster noodles.

SENSO *Italian* $$$
☎ 6225 3534; 21 Club St; ⏰ noon-2.30pm & 6.30-10.30pm; Ⓜ Chinatown; ♿ Ⓥ

There are hundreds of Italian restaurants in Singapore, but none can beat this restaurant in a former school for romantic atmosphere. Book a table in the court yard under the stars for maximum effect (and hope it doesn't rain).

SMITH ST HAWKER CENTRE
Hawker Centre $

Smith St; ⏰ 6pm till late; Ⓜ Chinatown; ♿

You can't quite beat dinner in the open air – and clearly thousands of people agree, which is why Smith St Hawker Centre is such a hit. Grab a table, order a barbecued seafood feast, an endless stream of cold Tigers, and your night is made.

Y DRINK

The shophouse renovation frenzy that has swept Chinatown has been a natural magnet for fashionable watering holes, which line Club St and Ann Siang Rd. The Tanjong Pagar area has been a long-standing centre for the gay night-scene, while the larger bars around the Far East Sq area attract a mainstream office crowd intent on serious drinking.

Y BACKSTAGE BAR *Bar*
☎ 6227 1712; 13A Trengganu St; ⏰ 7pm-2am; Ⓜ Chinatown

The balcony of this Chinatown gay bar is a great spot to chat, flirt with local lads, or just sit and watch the world go by. Dark lighting, comfortable seating and flat-screen monitors often playing classic films gives the interior an intimate feel. Entrance on Temple St.

Y BEAUJOLAIS WINE BAR
Wine Bar
☎ 6224 2227; 1 Ann Siang Hill; ⏰ 11am-midnight Mon-Thu, 11am-2am Fri, 6pm-2am Sat; Ⓜ Chinatown

A tiny, raffish bar in a barely renovated shophouse, Beaujolais is the perfect antidote to the large corporate entertainment venues that are consuming the city. The upstairs lounge is a gem.

Y KAZBAR *Pub*
☎ 6438 2975; 01-03, Capital Square Three; ⏰ 11.30am-midnight Mon-Fri, 5.30pm-midnight Sat; Ⓜ Raffles Place; ♿

Popular Middle Eastern–themed pub, with curtained nooks and

deep sofas inside and bar tables outside. Male office workers seem strangely drawn to the place: surely nothing to do with the comely belly dancer doing the rounds in the early evening – must be the dips and pita bread.

Y LE CARILLON DE L'ANGELUS Wine Bar

☎ 6423 0353; 24 Ann Siang Rd; ☾ noon-midnight Mon-Fri, 6pm-midnight Sat; Ⓜ Chinatown; ♿

The excellent wines do justice to the superb tiled interior of this French wine bar. Lovely though it is upstairs, our favourite spot is the comfy chairs and sofa downstairs in a private little nook facing the chalkboard wine list. The cheese platter is a must.

Y OOSTERS Gastropub

☎ 6438 3210; 25 Church St, 01-04, Capital Square Three; ☾ noon-midnight Mon-Fri, 5.30pm-midnight Sat; Ⓜ Raffles Place

All dark wood, brass and big windows, Oosters re-creates the cosy interior of a Belgian pub, with a wide range of beers (the Leffe Blonde on tap is a favourite) and hearty food. Try the mussels.

Y SÁ VANH BISTRO Bar

☎ 6323 0145; 47 Club St; ☾ meals noon-3pm & 6-11pm, bar noon-1am Mon-Thu, noon-2am Fri & Sat; Ⓜ Chinatown

Sá Vanh's soft candles shed light on dusky shadows as gorgeous svelte things flit by the fishpond and the water wall, expats sink into sunken lounges, platters of

---

TEA TIME

The very antithesis of the quick cuppa, traditional Chinese tea preparation is meant to impose a period of concentration, relaxation and reflection on the drinker.

> Warm pot and cups.
> Add tea to strainer in pot.
> Fill pot with hot water to rinse leaves, then pour out immediately into jug.
> Refill pot to brim.
> Drag lid across top of pot to remove bubbles, then place lid back.
> Pour hot water collected from rinsing process over the pot.
> Infuse for 60 seconds, then pour into jug to ensure even strength.
> Pour from jug to sniffing cups.
> Drinker pours tea from sniffing cup to drinking cup, then smells empty sniffing cup to evaluate aroma.
> Drink.
> Start process again, noting subtle differences in colour and flavour in subsequent brewing.

Ruqxana Vasnwala
Chef & cooking instructor, Cookery Magic

Why are Singaporeans so mad about food? The answer to this question will come to you through your senses only when you are 'in' Singapore. It will be felt through your senses of sight, sound, smell, touch and the finale – taste. It permeates through your soul. **Four must-try Singapore dishes and where to find them?** The nonya laksa at 328 Katong Laksa (p106), chicken rice at Tian Tian at the Maxwell Rd Hawker Centre (p59), roti prata, available at any of the coffee shops at Jalan Kayu, and chilli crab or pepper crab at Eng Seng (p107) on Joo Chiat Pl. **Best place for a romantic dinner?** Personally the most romantic dinner would be in a home with the meal cooked for you by your loved one, no matter how simple the meal is – a private candlelight dinner preferably in the garden. But in the absence of this scenario, I would suggest restaurants with good food and service, with privacy and the ambience of being close to nature. Hacienda (p126) is a good midrange choice. **Favourite hawker centre?** East Coast Lagoon (p107). It's right on the ocean!

Asian tapas make the rounds, and ambient tunes snake into the night – all under the heavy-lidded gaze of Buddha himself.

▼ TABOO *Nightclub*
☎ 6225 6256; 65/67 Neil Rd; ☽ 8pm-2am Wed & Thu, 10pm-3am Fri, 10pm-4am Sat

Hottest gay dance club on the scene (for the moment, at least), always packed with the requisite line-up of shirtless gyrators, dance-happy straight women and regular saucy themed nights.

▼ THE TERRACE *Bar*
☎ 6221 1694; www.screeningroom .com.sg; Level 5, 12 Ann Siang Rd; ☽ 6pm-2am Mon-Thu, 6pm-3am Fri & Sat; Ⓜ Chinatown

The views across Chinatown and the CBD from this intimate rooftop bar, part of the hip Screening Room (opposite), are superb. Bag a comfy couch on the periphery, kick the shoes off and have a shouting-into-each-other's-ears conversation over the sound system.

▼ THE TOUCAN *Pub*
☎ 6223 5950; 15 Duxton Hill; ☽ 11am-1am Mon-Thu, 11am-3am Fri, 3pm-3am Sat; Ⓜ Tanjong Pagar

Unique among Singapore's Irish pubs in that it has a proper beer garden: a lawn, wooden benches, big umbrellas, even a wishing well.

▼ W WINE BAR *Wine Bar*
☎ 6223 3886; www.wwinebar.sg; 11 Club St; ☽ 5pm-2am; Ⓜ Chinatown; ♿

Tiny, intimate, relaxed, low-lit – everything you could want in a pre- or postdinner wine bar. There are low tables and sofas and, of course, a huge list of around 300 wines.

★ PLAY

★ KENKO WELLNESS SPA *Spa*
☎ 6223 0303; www.kenko.com.sg; 199 South Bridge Rd; reflexology per 30min $33, massages per 30min $49; ☽ 10am-10pm; Ⓜ Chinatown; ♿

Kenko is the McDonald's of Singapore's spas with branches throughout the city, but there's nothing drive-through about its foot reflexology, romantic couples' sessions ($328 per 2½-hour session) or Chinese and Swedish massage (Chinese is more forceful, using pointy elbows).

★ LINE DANCING *Dance*
www.cldas.com; Fire Gate, Far East Sq, 70 Telok Ayer St; ☽ 7-10.30pm Fri; Ⓜ Raffles Place

Every Friday evening at 7pm, like clockwork, up go the speakers, people arrive, on go the uniforms, the hats and the boots, and commuters driving along Cross St are treated to the arcane pleasures

Expect enchanting city views from the top of the Screening Room, Chinatown

of public line dancing. If the lure is too strong, saunter up to the desk in the corner and pay $3 to join in.

⭐ THE SCREENING ROOM
Cinema
☎ 6221 1694; www.screeningroom
.com.sg; 12 Ann Siang Rd; ⏰ noon-2.30pm & 6pm-late; Ⓜ Chinatown; ♿
All-in-one entertainment venue comprising two bars, screening room, bistro and function room. The highlights, in a city swamped by mainstream Hollywood, are the sofa-filled movie rooms and the rooftop bar offering fantastic views across the district. Pay $75 for a Food & Film package.

⭐ URBAN FAIRWAYS
Virtual Golf
☎ 6327 8045; www.urbanfairways.com; 27 Club St; off-peak/peak per group of 1-4 people $125/150; ⏰ 7am-1am Mon-Fri, 7am-5pm Sat & Sun; Ⓜ Chinatown; ♿ ♿
Billing itself as Asia's first virtual-golf centre, offering players a virtual round on the world's top courses – all in air-conditioned comfort. Popular with corporate groups.

NEIGHBOURHOODS

COLONIAL DISTRICT & THE QUAYS

>COLONIAL DISTRICT & THE QUAYS

If Little India and Chinatown are the soul of Singapore, then the Colonial District (Civic District) is its heart and the Quays are its fancy hairdo.

Home of Singapore's most photographed buildings and vistas, the Colonial District is an area of such architectural richness that a treasure seems to appear at every turn (see Walking Tour, p144). The list of heritage structures is endless: Raffles Hotel, City Hall, the Singapore Art Museum, the National Museum and the Asian Civilisations Museum to name but a few. And increasingly, for a city that threatened to commit architectural suicide in the '60s and '70s, modern buildings such as the magnificent Esplanade are earning Singapore a cutting-edge reputation.

COLONIAL DISTRICT & THE QUAYS

◉ SEE
Asian Civilisations
  Museum 1 D3
at-Sunrice Global Chef
  Academy ....(see 28)
Esplanade - Theatres
  on the Bay (& Mall) 2 F5
Merlion 3 F6
National Museum of
  Singapore 4 D3
Peranakan Museum 5 D3
Singapore Art Museum ..6 E2

🛍 SHOP
Funan - The IT Mall 7 E4
Mothercare 8 G3
Robinsons 9 F4
Royal Selangor 10 C5
The Cathay 11 D2

🍴 EAT
Ah Teng's Bakery 12 F3
Coriander Leaf 13 C5

Equinox 14 F4
My Humble House ....(see 2)
No Signboard
  Seafood ....(see 2)
Pierside Kitchen &
  Bar 15 F6
Royal China 16 F3

🍸 DRINK
Actor's Bar 17 D5
Archipelago 18 D6
Bar & Billiard
  Room 19 F3
Brewerkz 20 C5
City Space ....(see 14)
Crazy Elephant 21 D5
Cuba Libre 22 C5
Harry's 23 E6
Mr Punch Winebar 24 F3
Paulaner Brauhaus 25 G4
Post Bar ....(see 15)
Rupee Room 26 C4
Southbridge Jazz @
  7atenine ....(see 2)

⭐ PLAY
Attica 27 C5
Black Box ....(see 28)
Drama Centre ....(see 28)
DXO ....(see 2)
Esplanade - Theatres
  on the Bay ....(see 2)
Fort Canning Centre 28 D3
G-Max Reserve
  Bungy 29 D5
Museum of Toys 30 F3
Singapore Dance
  Theatre ....(see 28)
Singapore Repertory
  Theatre 31 B4
The Arena 32 C4
The Arts House 33 E5
The Butter Factory 34 F6
Theatreworks ....(see 28)
Victoria Theatre &
  Concert Hall 35 E5
Willow Stream 36 F3

Please see over for map

Down by the riverside is where much of Singapore has its fun: enough bars, microbreweries, restaurants and nightclubs are strung along the Quays to keep you occupied for a year.

👁 SEE

👁 ASIAN CIVILISATIONS MUSEUM

☎ 6332 2982; www.acm.org.sg; 1 Empress Pl; adult/child $8/4; ⏳ 1pm-7pm Mon, 9am-7pm Tue-Thu, Sat & Sun, 9am-9pm Fri; Ⓜ Raffles Place; ♿

Housed in a magnificently restored 1865 building, the ACM is one of Singapore's icons and a must-see. Set over three levels, the 10 permanent exhibits explore traditional aspects of pan-Asian culture and civilisation, including all of Southeast Asia, China, India and Sri Lanka. The sheer scale of the museum is such that, for the uninitiated, the ACM Highlights guided tour (2pm Monday, 11am and 2pm Tuesday to Friday) is advisable – though it doesn't run from late December to early January.

👁 ESPLANADE – THEATRES ON THE BAY

☎ 6828 0377; www.esplanade.com; 1 Esplanade Dr; guided tours adult/child $10/8; ⏳ 10am-6pm; Ⓜ City Hall; ♿

The design of Esplanade – Theatres on the Bay was the subject of much controversy when it was first built

Istana Park

Cuppage Centre

Grange Rd

Somerset

PUB Building

Penang Rd

Orchard Rd

Penang Rd

Devonshire Rd

Exeter Rd

Eber Rd

Oxley Rd

Killiney Rd

Clemenceau Ave

Penang La

Plaza Singapura

Oldham La

Handy Rd

11

Mt Sophia Rd

Wilkie Rd

Edinburgh Rd

Adis Rd

Dhoby Ghaut

Orchard Rd

Bras Basah Park

Fort Canning Tunnel

4

See Orchard Rd Map pp40-1

Lloyd Rd

Oxley Rise

Oxley Wk

Fort Canning Rd

Canning Walk

Canning Rise

28

1

5

0   400 m
0   0.2 miles

Kim Yam Rd

River Valley Cl

Martin Rd

Rodyk St

Saiboo St

Nanson Rd

Mohamed Sultan Rd

Unity St

Merbau Rd

Clemenceau Ave

Tank Rd

31

Liang Ct

Ord Bridge

26

River Valley Rd

Read St

32

10

27   22

13

21

Fort Canning Reservoir

Fort Canning Park

Singapore Philatelic Museum

Hill St

High Cent

29

Coleman

North Boat Qu

Havelock Rd

Jl Minyak

Magazine Rd

Cumming St

Merchant Rd

20

Read Bridge

Clarke Quay

Riverwalk Galleria

York Hill

Central Expressway

Pearl's Hill Rd

Havelock Rd

Havelock Square

North Canal Rd

Eu Tong Sen St

Carpenter St

Hongkong St

Circular

18

Pearl's Hill City Park

Pearl's Hill Reservoir

See Chinatown & the CBD Map pp52-3

Park Cres

Upper Hokien St

Upper Pickering St

Church St

Hong Lim Park

Pidemco Centre

George St

Synagogue St

South Bridge Rd

OCBC Centre

See Little India & Arab Quarter
Map pp84-5

GETTING THERE & AROUND
> **MRT** – The North South line from Dhoby Ghaut–City Hall–Raffles Place is the best means of traversing the area.
> **Bus** – 174 runs along Bras Basah Rd, then turns down North Bridge Rd to the river.

One of Southeast Asia's most stunning pieces of architecture, the Esplanade was created to announce Singapore's arrival on the world arts scene – and also as a challenge to the city's deep-seated conservatism. It succeeded on both counts, with a year-round program of opera, classical music, jazz, theatre, dance and a host of fringe events. Taking a guided tour – or a self-guided iTour using an electronic guide – is a great way of exploring this iconic structure. The website lists upcoming performances.

🅒 NATIONAL MUSEUM OF SINGAPORE
☎ 6332 3659; www.nationalmuseum.sg; 93 Stamford Rd; adult/child $10/5, after 6pm free; 🕙 10am-8pm; Ⓜ Dhoby Ghaut/City Hall then walk
Imaginative, prodigiously stocked and brilliantly designed, the National Museum is good enough to deserve two visits. Among the permanent exhibits are the Singapore History Gallery and four other galleries based on Singaporean culture. There are also rotating and visiting exhibits ranging in theme from ancient history to pop culture. The grand architecture alone makes it worth a visit.

🅒 PERANAKAN MUSEUM
☎ 6332 7591; www.peranakanmuseum.sg; 39 Armenian St; adult/child $6/3; 🕙 9.30am-7pm, from 1pm Mon, till 9pm Fri; Ⓜ City Hall; ♿

FLY EYES AND DURIANS
The Esplanade theatres, designed by a twin team of UK and local architects, cost a staggering $600 million and are built entirely on reclaimed land. The structure sits on a vast slab of rubber and, unusually, was constructed from the inside out. Not just visually impressive, the main Concert Hall inside is acoustically spectacular, containing a three-piece acoustic canopy and 84 computer-controlled doors and flaps hidden behind the hall's mahogany ribs that can make minute adjustments to the reverberations. The controversial exterior, variously compared to durians, fly eyes and honeycomb, is encased in aluminium shades set at various angles to maximise natural light while shielding the interior from the harsh sun. At night, it comes into its own, when interior lighting makes the whole building glow a beautiful green.

This beautiful new museum is home to both permanent and rotating visits designed to illuminate and promote the culture and colour of the Peranakan people. Lots of hands-on stuff for the kiddies as well. Free admission from 7pm to 9pm on Fridays.

RAFFLES HOTEL
☎ 6337 1886; www.raffleshotel.com; 1 Beach Rd; Ⓜ City Hall; ♿

Whatever ostentatious modern projects Singapore undertakes now or in the future, Raffles Hotel will likely always be its most famous landmark. There's just something about the sight of that snow-white facade, the brushed-gravel drive, the Sikh doorman, the whispers of history. Astonishing to think it was scheduled for demolition in 1987, before a $160 million facelift restored it to glory.

SINGAPORE ART MUSEUM
☎ 6332 3222; www.nhb.gov.sg/sam; 71 Bras Basah Rd; adult/child $8/4, noon-2pm Mon-Fri & 6-9pm Fri free; ⏱ 10am-7pm Sat-Thu, 10am-9pm Fri; Ⓜ Dhoby Ghaut, City Hall; ♿

Watch the Singapore skyline slowly roll by from the cabin of the Singapore Flyer (p73)

Lim Chen Sian
Archaeologist & heritage buff

Best place to stroll to check out authentic colonial era architecture? The museum district around Stamford Rd and Bras Basah is good, as is the Civic District by the mouth of Singapore River. I like walking around the many narrow lanes and alleys off Serangoon Rd, especially in the early evening. The crumbling squat colonial-era shophouses give a great feel of what the city was like under colonial rule, with bustling street vendors and commerce. **Best museum for history buffs?** The Asian Civilisations Museum (p67), the National Museum (p70) and the Peranakan Museum (p70) are the flagships, but my all-time favourites are the Chinatown Heritage Centre (p51) and the Civil Defence Gallery. **Best place in town to see examples of pre-colonial Singapore?** The Fort Canning (p39) archaeological dig site – a small outdoor archaeological display is erected over the place. Loads of artefacts have been recovered from the site dating from the 14th century. **Is a Singaporean Sling really Singaporean?** Not in my opinion! I would say that Ice Milo is a more true Singaporean heritage beverage, and you can get it cheap at any coffee shop!

Magnificently restored, the Singapore Art Museum houses one of the finest collections of Southeast Asian art, both traditional and contemporary, and also hosts frequent travelling exhibitions. Major local artists such as Lim Tze Peng and Chen Chong Swee are also represented.

◎ SINGAPORE FLYER
☎ 6333 3311; www.singaporeflyer.com.sg; Raffles Ave; ⏱ 8.30am-10.30pm; adult/child $29.50/20.65 Ⓜ City Hall, then shuttle bus from St Andrew's Cathedral, bus 105, 111, 133
This is the world's largest observation wheel (beating the London Eye by 30m) and one of the key Marina Bay developments, alongside the Marina Bay Sands casino resort and the Gardens by the Bay. Set in lush gardens, the 30-minute ride is best done on a clear blue day, or on a clear night, when the lights of Indonesia and Malaysia frame the spectacular pan-Singapore views.

🄰 SHOP

🄰 FUNAN DIGITALIFE MALL *IT*
☎ 6336 8327; www.funan.com.sg; 109 North Bridge Rd; ⏱ 10.30am-9.30pm; Ⓜ City Hall; ♿
Tech mall of choice for people who prefer to pay a bit more for branded products and cast-iron guarantees, rather than brave the aisles of Sim Lim Sq (p89). **Challenger Superstore** (☎ 6339 9008; Level 6) is the best one-stop shop for all IT needs.

STREET SCULPTURE
Singapore is dappled with a healthy crop of public sculpture by acclaimed local and international artists. Check these out:

> **Abundance** (Map pp68–9, G4) by Sun Yu Li – Suntec City
> **Between Sea & Sky** (Map pp68–9, G4) by Olivier Strehelle – Marina Mandarin Hotel, 6 Raffles Blvd
> **Bird** (Map pp52–3, G2) by Fernando Botero – UOB Plaza, Boat Quay
> **Homage to Newton** (Map pp52–3, G2) by Salvador Dali – UOB Plaza, Boat Quay
> **LOVE** (Map pp40–1, H5) by Robert Indiana – Penang Rd
> **Millennium** (Map pp68–9, E6) by Victor Tan – Empress Pl
> **Reclining Figures** (Map pp52–3, F2) by Henry Moore – OCBC Centre
> **Seed sculptures** (Map pp68–9, G5) by Singaporean artist Han Sai Por – Esplanade waterfront garden
> **Six Brushstrokes** (Map pp68–9, H4) by Roy Lichtenstein – Millenia Walk, 9 Raffles Blvd
> **First Generation** (Map pp52–3, H2) by Chong Fat Cheong – Cavenagh Bridge

NEIGHBOURHOODS

COLONIAL DISTRICT & THE QUAYS

COLONIAL DISTRICT & THE QUAYS

▣ ROYAL SELANGOR *Crafts*
☎ 6268 9600; 01-01 Clarke Quay;
🕙 9am-9pm; Ⓜ Clarke Quay
If Uncle Jim has always craved his
own personalised tankard, here's
your chance to get it for him.
Indulge the short pewter-smithery
demonstration, then admire the
range of other articles, from jewellery to hip flasks, Malaysia's pewter
specialists turn out.

🍴 EAT

🍴 AH TENGS BAKERY *Cafe* $$
☎ 6412 1100; Raffles Hotel Complex,
1 Beach Rd; 🕙 7.30am-10pm;
Ⓜ City Hall; ♿
Perfect spot for a coffee-and-
pastry breakfast, evoking a more
genteel age with its marble-
topped tables and clinking china.

TEH WHAT?

Forget your lattes, mochas and macchia-
tos. Before taking on a Singapore-style
coffeeshop, you need to learn a whole
different lingo.
> **kopi** – coffee with condensed milk
> **teh** – tea with condensed milk
> **kopi-o/teh-o** – black coffee/tea
  with sugar
> **kopi-c/teh-c** – coffee/tea with
  evaporated milk and sugar
> **kopi-peng/teh-peng** – iced cof-
  fee/tea
> **teh tarik** – literally 'pulled tea', a
  sweet spiced Indian tea

The dim sum makes a pretty
decent afternoon snack, too.

🍴 CORIANDER LEAF
Asian Fusion $$
☎ 6732 3354; www.corianderleaf.com;
02-03, 3A Merchant Court, River Valley Rd;
🕙 noon-2pm & 6.30-10pm Mon-Fri, 6.30-
10.30pm Sat; Ⓜ Clarke Quay; ♿ Ⓥ
An exercise in fusing the tiny mor-
sels and artistic sauce (or should
we say jus?) dribbles of nouvelle
cuisine with traditional Asian flavours. Largely, it works, though the
menu can be a little disorientating
(hmm...Scottish salmon, miso cod
or Thai barramundi?). Also runs
highly regarded cooking courses.

🍴 EQUINOX *International* $$$
☎ 6837 3322; Level 70, Swissôtel,
the Stamford, 2 Stamford Rd; 🕙 noon-
2.30pm & 7-11pm; Ⓜ City Hall; ♿ Ⓥ
If it wasn't for the incredible views,
this might be rated an average
restaurant. As it is, 70 floors up you
won't care that the food is good,
but not great. Book ahead, ask for
a windowside table and chances
are you'll spend so much time
looking outside you'll forget to eat
anyway. After dinner, head to City
Space (p76) to continue gawping.

🍴 LEI GARDEN *Chinese* $$$
☎ 6339 3822; 01-24, CHIJMES, 30 Vic-
toria St; 🕙 11.30am-3pm & 6-9.30pm;
Ⓜ City Hall; ♿

Firm favourite for fancy Chinese dinners, the seafood at Lei is particularly well done (try the cod), but the roast pork also attracts a loyal following. Service can be patchy, so avoid when extremely crowded.

🍴 MY HUMBLE HOUSE
Chinese $$$
☎ 6423 1881; www.tunglok.com; 02-27, Esplanade Mall, 8 Raffles Ave; ⏰ 11.45am-3pm & 6.30-11pm; Ⓜ City Hall; ♿

We're not sure if the name is ironic, but humble is not the first word that comes to mind when you clap eyes on the outlandish decor (designed by Chinese artist Zhang Jin Jie) and contemplate set lunches with names such as 'The Wind Wafts Above the Shoulder' and 'Memories of that Spring'. A memorable experience.

🍴 PIERSIDE KITCHEN & BAR
Fusion Seafood $$$
☎ 6438 0400; 01-01, One Fullerton, 1 Fullerton Rd; ⏰ noon-3pm & 6-10pm; Ⓜ Raffles Place; ♿

Pierside's minimalist alfresco stylings earn the Singapore stamp of cool. Mirrored walls double the area the waiters need to cover – they glide around distributing plates of snapper pie, cumin-spiced crab cakes and lobster gumbo to well-heeled diners.

🍴 ROYAL CHINA *Chinese* $$$
☎ 6338 3363; 03-09, Raffles Hotel, 1 Beach Rd; ⏰ noon-3pm & 6-10.30pm; Ⓜ City Hall; ♿ Ⓥ

An excellent spot for afternoon dim sum, though you'll likely need to reserve a table. Have a light breakfast and fill up on scallop dumplings, crispy duck and lobster noodles.

🍴 TIFFIN ROOM *Indian* $$$
☎ 6431 6156; Lobby, Raffles Hotel, 1 Beach Rd; ⏰ 7am-7pm; Ⓜ City Hall; ♿ Ⓥ

The very name evokes pith helmets, linen suits and parasols, and the elegant interior only reinforces the image. Open all day, but best visited for the dinner buffet starting at 7pm, which is something close to curry heaven, though you may need to be carried out after.

🍸 DRINK
🍸 ACTOR'S BAR *Bar*
☎ 6535 3270; 13 South Bridge Rd; 6pm-3am Mon-Thu, 6pm-4am Fri & Sat; Ⓜ Clarke Quay

Every night is open-mic night at the Actor's Bar, where customers are given the opportunity to get up and play music on one of the several assembled instruments laid out for jamming. Just the place to let your inner Elvis out!

NEIGHBOURHOODS

COLONIAL DISTRICT & THE QUAYS

ARCHIPELAGO *Microbrewery*
☎ 6327 8408; www.archipelagobrewery
.com; 79 Circular Rd; 🕙 3pm-1am
Sun-Thu, 4pm-3am Fri & Sat; Ⓜ Raffles
Place; ♿
Hopping merrily on the Singapore microbrewery bandwagon, Archipelago has embarked on an aggressive campaign to sell its Asian-accented beers in other bars across the island, but this, its flagship pub on a Y-junction in mildly seedy Circular Rd, is still the best place to enjoy them.

BAR & BILLIARD ROOM *Bar*
☎ 6412 1816; www.raffleshotel.com;
1 Beach Rd; 🕙 11.30am-10pm;
Ⓜ City Hall; ♿
Forget the Long Bar, this is the quintessential Raffles drinking hole. Gentle lighting, genteel service, the clack of billiard balls, and a breezy verandah next to the spot where Somerset Maugham used to set up his typewriter.

BREWERKZ *Microbrewery*
☎ 6438 7438; 01-05, Riverside Point
Centre, 30 Merchant Rd; 🕙 noon-
midnight Sun-Thu, noon-1am Fri & Sat;
Ⓜ Clarke Quay; ♿
The first among Singapore's crop of microbreweries and still among the best – and certainly the biggest. Some might prefer the more intimate surroundings of its rivals, but Brewerkz manages

to combine large scale with great service – something of a rarity in Singapore. The beers are uniformly superb, and lunchtime boozers will find the $4.99 pints from noon to 3pm an invitation to dispense with other plans for the day.

CITY SPACE *Lounge Bar*
☎ 6837 3322; Level 70, Swissôtel, the
Stamford, 2 Stamford Rd; 🕙 5pm-1am;
Ⓜ City Hall; ♿
Deep armchairs, light jazz, Cuban cigars, fortified wines and stunning night-time views over the island – this is the kind of place that makes you wish you owned a velvet smoking jacket.

CUBA LIBRE *Bar*
☎ 6338 8982; 01-13, Block B, Clarke
Quay; 🕙 6pm-1am Sun-Thu, 6pm-3am
Fri & Sat; Ⓜ Clarke Quay ; ♿
Follow the sound of trilling trumpets for a night of mojitos, live salsa and merengue music and dancing at this raucous Cuban-themed club. Looking to drink like Papa Hemingway? Buy one get one free on selected drinks is in effect from 6pm to 9pm daily.

HARRY'S BAR *Pub*
☎ 6538 3029; 28 Boat Quay; 🕙 11am-
1am Sun-Thu, 11am-2am Fri & Sat;
Ⓜ Raffles Place; ♿
The original and best. Harry's is a classic financial-district hang-out

that gained moderate infamy as the haunt of Barings-buster Nick Leeson and remains a favourite for its jovial atmosphere and great live jazz, blues and R&B.

▼ MR PUNCH WINEBAR
Wine Bar

☎ 6334 5155; 26 Seah St; 4pm-midnight Mon-Thu, 4pm-2am Fri & Sat; Ⓜ City Hall or Bugis, then walk; ♿

Soft jazz, beautiful views of the surrounding skyline and scores of vintage enamel advertising signs from around the world (some dating as far back as the 19th century) make this intimate space a lovely spot to unwind with a few drinks at the end of the day. Mr Punch is located on the rooftop of the Museum of Toys (p80) and makes it – oddly enough – almost child-friendly, a rare thing indeed for a place serving spirits. There's a decent menu, and even a good selection of alcohol-free drinks, should you decide on a post-Museum visit.

▼ PAULANER BRAUHAUS
Microbrewery

☎ 6883 2572; www.paulaner.com.sg; 01-01, Times Square, Millenia Walk, 9 Raffles Blvd; ☽ 11.30am-1am Sun-Thu, till 2am Fri & Sat; Ⓜ City Hall

Wear your best pastel-striped shirt or power dress to mix with the business crowd downing highly addictive German beers at this

convention-centre microbrewery. The inconvenient location at soulless Suntec City means that once you've made the effort to get here, you might as well dig in for the long haul. Two more please, fraulein.

▼ POST BAR *Bar*

☎ 6733 8388; Fullerton Hotel, 1 Fullerton Rd; ☽ noon-2am; Ⓜ Raffles Place; ♿

Retaining the original post-office ceiling, decked out with modern sculptures and some decidedly futuristic underfloor lighting, Post Bar exudes class without snobbery and mixes an outstanding mojito. Worth dressing up for.

NEIGHBOURHOODS

COLONIAL DISTRICT & THE QUAYS

Y RUPEE ROOM *Bar*
☎ 6334 2455; www.harrys.com.sg
/Rupee.htm; 01-15, the Foundry, Clarke
Quay; ⏰ 5pm-4am; Ⓜ Clarke Quay; ♿

You've been practising those
shoulder shakes in your bedroom
for months, now it's time to don
the nylon shirt, do up a couple
of buttons, stick on the fake
moustache and get to it yah? For
a night of pure fun and silliness,
the Bollywood beats here are hard
to top. A $15 cover charge applies
Friday and Saturday.

Y SOUTHBRIDGE JAZZ @
7ATENINE *Jazz Bar, Bistro*
☎ 6338 0789; 01-10/12 Esplanade Mall;
5pm-1am Sun-Thu, 5pm-2am Fri & Sat;
Ⓜ City Hall

THE SINGAPORE SLING
It's a mystery to us why anyone would
drink cough syrup for enjoyment, but
evidently many people love this famous
cocktail, invented at Raffles Hotel by
barman Ngiam Tong Boon, so here's
the recipe:
> 30mL gin
> 15mL cherry brandy
> 120mL pineapple juice (or soda)
> 15mL lime juice
> 10mL Cointreau
> 10mL Benedictine herbal liqueur
> 15mL Angostura bitters

Shake with ice, decant into highball glass,
then decorate with cherry. Err...yum?

Run by the same folks in charge of
the legendary Jazz @ Southbridge,
Singapore's most happening
(and only) jazz club has found
a snazzier home in the shadow
of the Esplanade. Decadent
cocktails and fabulous jazz are on
the menu nightly. In addition to
imported acts the club also has a
resident quartet playing sultry jazz
standards along with occasional
improv. The attached restaurant
serves excellent continental
cuisine.

PLAY

☆ ATTICA *Nightclub*
☎ 6333 9973; www.attica.com.sg;
01-12, Clarke Quay; ⏰ 5pm-3am Sun-
Tue & Thu, till 4am Wed, Fri & Sat;
Ⓜ Clarke Quay

Attica has secured a loyal following
among Singapore's notoriously
fickle clubbers, modelling itself on
New York's hippest clubs but los-
ing the attitude somewhere over
the Pacific. The outdoor section is
mostly colonised by 30-something
expats, who find all the noisy
dancing kids inside a bit too much.
A $28 cover charge on Fridays and
Saturdays includes two drinks.

☆ CRAZY ELEPHANT
Blues Bar
☎ 6337 7859; www.crazyelephant.com;
01-03, Clarke Quay; ⏰ 5pm-2am Sun-Thu,
till 3am Fri & Sat; Ⓜ Clarke Quay; ♿

BEER TODAY, GONE TOMORROW

If you find yourself wandering around cursing because some bar or restaurant we said was superb has vanished into thin air, bear in mind that Singapore's night scene is notoriously erratic. The law in Singapore gives minimal protection to tenants, and often the demise of a bar will be the result of a dispute with the landlord, rather than its unpopularity.

If the remodelled Clarke Quay is a collection of eager-faced college kids, then Crazy Elephant is the crusty bloke in the corner watching them out of the corner of his eye and shaking his head. One of Singapore's oldest, trustiest live-music venues, this is the place to ditch all that electronic nonsense and listen to some serious, loud rock and blues.

⭐ DXO *Music, Comedy*
☎ 6582 4896; www.dxo.com.sg; 01-13F Esplanade Mall; Sun-Thu 6pm-2am, Fri & Sat 9pm-4am; Ⓜ City Hall, then walk; ♿
This swank and sexy multipurpose club located on Esplanade Mall hosts bands, international DJs, and even stand-up comedians (thanks to a time-share agreement with the Singapore branch of the Comedy Club Asia; see www. thecomedyclub.asia).

⭐ ESPLANADE – THEATRES ON THE BAY *Theatre*
☎ 6828 8377; www.esplanade.com; 1 Esplanade Dr; guided tours adult/child $10/8; ⏰ 10am-6pm; Ⓜ City Hall; ♿
Where to begin? In the outstanding Concert Hall, the world-class theatre, the host of smaller performance spaces? The Esplanade roused Singapore from its artistic coma and placed it firmly at the centre of the Asian arts world. There are more than a thousand performances in here every year, so there's no excuse for missing a chance to visit.

⭐ G-MAX REVERSE BUNGY *Thrill Ride*
☎ 6338 1146; Clarke Quay; $45 (both rides $60); ⏰ 3pm-midnight Sun-Thu, 2pm-3.30am Fri & Sat ; Ⓜ Clarke Quay
Flying upwards into the air at 200km/h inside a plastic pod attached to some elastic bands? Something tells us this is a Kiwi invention. A few Clarke Quay beers might improve your courage to have a go, but your stomach might not agree. Less terrifying is the neighbouring giant swing.

⭐ GUINNESS THEATRE *Theatre*
☎ 6337 7535; www.substation.org; 45 Armenian St; ⏰ box office noon-8.30pm Mon-Fri & 2hr before shows; Ⓜ City Hall

DRAMA QUEENS

Singapore's more dynamic and contemporary theatre groups produce both edgy and more accessible works at various venues around town. They often struggle for audiences and funds, but their undoubted passion keeps them alive. Banners advertising shows are usually plastered around town, or check listings in local magazines and newspapers. Groups include **Theatreworks** (www.theatreworks.org.sg), the **Theatre Practice** (www.ttp.org.sg), Singapore's sexiest and often most daring company, **Wild Rice** (www.wildrice.com.sg) and cutting-edge improvisational group **Cake** (www.caketheatre.com).

Part of the Substation experimental-arts complex, this small theatre (painted Irish-stout black) promotes works by emerging local artists. Many shows here are free, some have ticket prices. There are regular workshops for poetry, painting and suchlike as well.

⭐ MUSEUM OF TOYS *Museum*
☎ 6339 0660; www.emint.com; 26 Seah St; adult/child $15/7.50; 🕙 9.30am-6.30pm; Ⓜ City Hall or Bugis, then walk; ♿ ♿
This four-floor museum features an international collection of vintage toys as well as collectibles ranging from figurines to political propaganda. The lobby shop

is a great place to stock up on whimsical toys for the little ones back home.

⭐ SINGAPORE REPERTORY THEATRE *Theatre*
☎ 6733 8166; www.srt.com.sg; DBS Arts Centre, 20 Merbau Rd; tickets $30-80; 🚌 33, 54, 139, 195
At the bigwig of the Singapore theatre scene, expect to see repertory standards such as *Death of a Salesman* and *The Glass Menagerie*, as well as modern local works.

⭐ SINGAPORE SYMPHONY ORCHESTRA *Classical Music*
☎ 6348 5555; www.sso.org.sg; Esplanade Theatre, 1 Esplanade Dr; Ⓜ Raffles Place
The outstanding SSO likes its venues grand – it plays regularly at its Esplanade home and also at the splendid Victoria Concert Hall (Map pp68–9). Its most memorable of performances is on the Symphony Stage in the Singapore Botanic Gardens (p117).

⭐ THE ARENA *Live Music*
☎ 6338 3158; www.thearenalive.com.sg; 01-08, 3B Clarke Quay; 🕙 5pm-4am Tue-Thu, 5pm-5am Fri-Sun; Ⓜ Clarke Quay; ♿
Touted as the largest live-music space in Singapore, this slick venue wheels out international bands and DJs for short residences or

one-off gigs. Expect danceable mainstream top 40, hip-hop and house to a cashed-up crowd.

⭐ THE BUTTER FACTORY *Club*
☎ 6333 8243; www.thebutterfactory.com; 1 Fullerton Rd; ⏰ 10pm-3am Wed, 10pm-4am Fri & Sat; Ⓜ Clarke Quay

In a new location across from the Fullerton Hotel, the Butter Factory and its decor still offer a unique blend of cyber-future meets cartoonish whimsy. Comfy-couched chill-out spots, dance-floors and a good bar make this a decent night spot. Check the website for cover charges.

⭐ WILLOW STREAM *Spa*
☎ 6431 5600; Level 6, Fairmont Hotel, 80 Bras Basah; ⏰ massage 9am-10pm, fitness centre 5.30am-11pm; Ⓜ City Hall

Connected to the Fairmont Hotel (and formerly known as Amrita Spa), Willow Stream offers top-of-the-range spa treatments, including back massages from $79 and facials from $140. There's also a state-of-the-art gymnasium.

⭐ ZOUK *Nightclub*
☎ 6738 2988; www.zoukclub.com.sg; 17 Jiak Kim St; entry $20-35; ⏰ Zouk & Phuture 8pm-3.30am Wed, Fri & Sat, Wine Bar 6pm-3.30am Mon-Sun; 🚕 taxi

Ibiza-inspired Zouk is a regular destination for globe-trotting DJs. Five bars, 2000 capacity and a roomy dance floor – there's guaranteed bar access and plenty of space to cut the rug. Minimum-age entry is 21 for women, 23 for men.

Clarke Quay is home to bars, nightclubs, restaurants and a comedy club

COLONIAL DISTRICT & THE QUAYS

>LITTLE INDIA & THE ARAB QUARTER

The closest you'll get to seeing what old Singapore city was like, Little India is a ramshackle, colourful, disorderly sort of place, where life tumbles along with an unfettered liveliness largely lost from the rest of the city. Goods crowd the five-foot ways, bhangra thuds from speakers, shopkeepers still paint signs on concrete pillars, irresistible food smells waft into the street and men clad in *dhoti* (loincloth) lounge around the market gossiping. It's like India with all the confronting bits taken out.

The quieter Arab Quarter, dominated by the large Sultan Mosque, has developed a low-key scene of its own, assisted by the pedestrianisation of Bussorah St. A clutch of Middle Eastern eateries and new shops has revitalised the area – and at night the fragrant smoke of *shisha* (flavoured

LITTLE INDIA & THE ARAB QUARTER

◉ SEE
Kuan Im Thong Hood
　Cho Temple 1 C7
Nanyang Academy of
　Fine Arts 2 B7
Sri Srinivasa Perumal
　Temple 3 D3
Sri Veeramakaliamman
　Temple 4 C5
Sultan Mosque 5 D6
The Gateway 6 D7
Trippies & Children's
　Little Museum .... (see 19)

◉ SHOP
Basheer Graphic Books ... 7 C8
Bugis St Market 8 C7
Fu Lou Shou 9 C7
Golden Mile Complex ...(see 31)
Haji Lane Shops 10 D7
Indian Classical Music
　Centre 11 C6

Indian Handicraft
　Centre 12 C6
Khan Mohamed Bhoy
　& Sons 13 C5
Little Shophouse .... (see 19)
Melor's Curios 14 E7
Mustafa Centre 15 C4
Parco Bugis Junction ... 16 D7
Sim Lim Sq 17 C6
Sungei Rd Thieves
　Market 18 D6
Tekka Centre .... (see 35)
Trippies & Children's
　Little Museum 19 E7

◉ EAT
Ananda Bhavan 20 B5
Ananda Bhavan 21 C4
Ananda Bhavan 22 B6
Ananda Bhavan 23 B6
Andhra Curry 24 B5
Anjappar 25 C4

Banana Leaf Apolo 26 B5
Café Le Caire 27 E7
Chettinadu 28 B5
French Stall 29 D3
Gandhi 30 B5
Golden Mile Complex ... 31 F6
Masala Hut 32 B5
Red Place's BBQ 33 E7
Sungei Rd Laksa 34 D5
Tekka Centre 35 B5

◉ DRINK
BluJaz Café 36 E7
Going Om 37 D7
Prince of Wales 38 C6
Thai Disco 39 F6

◉ PLAY
Climb Asia 40 D3
Rex Theatre 41 B6

Please see over for map

tobacco) pipes mingles with the charcoal smoke along the dimly lit streets to give it a character all its own.

Towards the city centre, Bugis has been taken over by Singapore's largest street market, and is the place to go for cheap clothes, shoes and accessories.

SEE

Little India is not renowned for the kind of attractions that fill brochures – the Colonial District has cornered the market on postcard sights – but it is a neighbourhood that warrants aimless wandering. Strolling through the narrow side streets with no fixed destination and watching life unfold is one of the great pleasures to be had here.

KUAN IM THONG HOOD CHO TEMPLE
178 Waterloo St; 6am-6.15pm; Bugis;
Dedicated to Kuan Yin, goddess of mercy, this is one of Singapore's busiest temples. Flower sellers, fortune tellers and incense-wielding devotees swarm around the entrance and rub the belly of the large bronze Buddha Maitreya nearby.

SRI SRINIVASA PERUMAL TEMPLE
6298 5771; 397 Serangoon Rd; 6.30am-noon & 6-9pm; Farrer Park;
Dating from 1855, this is one of the city's most important temples.

If you're here in February for the Thaipusam Festival (p24), the procession of devotees, with spikes and skewers driven through their bodies, begins under the temple's *gopuram* (entrance tower).

SRI VEERAMAKALIAMMAN TEMPLE
6293 4634; 141 Serangoon Rd; 5.15am-12.15pm & 4pm-9.15pm; Little India
One of Little India's more colourful temples, this place is dedicated to the goddess Kali, bloodthirsty consort of Shiva, who is usually depicted wearing a necklace of skulls and disembowelling unfortunate humans.

GETTING THERE & AROUND
> **MRT** – The North East Line from Little India to Farrer Park gets you from one end of the area to the other.
> **Bus** – 23, 64, 65, 66 and 147 run the length of Serangoon Rd. 48 runs from Little India MRT on Bukit Timah Rd to the Arab Quarter (get off on Ophir Rd).

NEIGHBOURHOODS

LITTLE INDIA & THE ARAB QUARTER

Visit Singapore's largest mosque, the grand Sultan Mosque

 SULTAN MOSQUE
☎ 6293 4405; 3 Muscat St;
🕒 9am-4pm; Ⓜ Bugis
Singapore's largest mosque and
the spiritual focal point for the
neighbourhood since the days
when it was the embarkation point
for Mecca-bound pilgrims. The
current magnificent, imposing
building (designed, interestingly, by
an Irishman) dates from 1928, but a
mosque has stood there since 1825.

🛍 SHOP
Little India and the Arab Quarter
are heaven for browsers and
mall-haters – look, real shops, run
by real shop owners, and barely
a whiff of air-con or polished
marble! Little India brims with
gold shops, textiles, handicrafts,
food, music and art. In the Arab
Quarter, Arab St is well known for
its textiles and carpets, pedestri-

BUSSORAH STREET

A few years ago, it was decided that Bussorah St was the ideal location for an 'alternative lifestyle hub'. Since then, this tiled, tree-lined pedestrianised strip has become one of the city's most appealing streets, filled with handicraft shops, a backpacker hostel and several cafes, all in the shadow of the Sultan Mosque (from which calls to prayer resonate throughout the day). Among the shops worth checking out are the Little Shophouse, which specialises in the intricate and beautiful art of Peranakan beadwork, and the Javanese arts and crafts at Melor's Curios.

anised Bussorah St has become a mildly bohemian enclave of knick-knacks, galleries and spas, while the back street of Haji Lane houses some hip boutiques and secondhand shops. New Bugis St has been turned into a two-storey street market likely to swallow teenagers whole.

📷 BASHEER GRAPHIC BOOKS *Graphic Books*

☎ 6336 0810; www.basheergraphic .com; 04-19, Bras Basah Complex; 10am-8.30pm Mon-Sat, 11am-6.30pm Sun; Ⓜ Bugis

Located inside of the Bras Basah Complex (known as 'Book City' locally), Basheer is a veritable cornucopia of graphic books. The shop also does a brisk mail-order

business, so if you're mid-travel and want to have something mailed to you, staff are happy to help.

📷 BUGIS STREET MARKET
Street Market

Victoria St; 🕙 **11am-10pm;** Ⓜ **Bugis**
Once Singapore's most infamous sleaze pit, this is now its largest street market, filled with cheap clothes, shoes, accessories, manicurists, food stalls and, in a nod to its past, a sex shop. You'll even find (gasp) the occasional knock-off.

📷 GOLDEN MILE COMPLEX
Food

5001 Beach Rd; 🕙 **9am-9pm;** Ⓜ **Bugis, Lavender**
This is Thailand: the whole human circus wrapped up, packaged

HAJI LANE

It's the kind of place you'd walk past without a second thought — a narrow, dingy lane with crumbling, graffiti-covered walls and no evident appeal. But Haji Lane is becoming a place of pilgrimage for Singapore's hipsters and fashionistas who insist on wearing originals from smaller shops, and those who wouldn't be caught dead inside an Orchard Rd Mall. Boutiques come and go rapidly (thanks in part to rising rents), but shops along the street tend to cater along the lines of hip, retro and street chic.

inside an unattractive shopping centre and transported to Singapore (minus the motorbikes running you down on the pavement). This is the place to come for Thai groceries, including all the essential roots, leaves and pastes you'll struggle to find anywhere else. Stay for lunch or dinner (see p92).

☐ **INDIAN CLASSICAL MUSIC CENTRE** *Music*
☎ **6291 0187; 26 Clive St;** ⊙ **10am-8pm Mon-Sat, 10am-4pm Sun;** Ⓜ **Little India**
A tiny shop filled with sitars, tabla and all manner of bells both wearable and shakeable. Buy CDs to play along to, or sign up for music lessons.

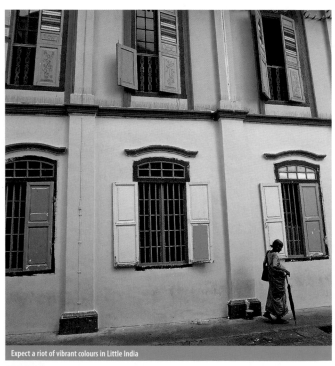
Expect a riot of vibrant colours in Little India

🏛 INDIAN HANDICRAFT CENTRE *Handicrafts, Furniture*
☎ 6392 0769; 2 Dalhousie Lane;
🕑 9am-9pm; Ⓜ Little India

The best place to browse for all things homely and Indian, from cushions to statues to furniture – this place has everything. A lot of larger items aren't displayed, so if you're looking for something in particular, ask the friendly owner.

🏛 KHAN MOHAMED BHOY & SONS *Food*
☎ 6293 6191; 20 Cuff Rd; 🕑 8am-8.30pm; Ⓜ Little India

You don't have to see this store to find it. Follow your nose to what may be the last traditional spice-grinding shop in Singapore. Plastic garbage bins full of dried bell chillies crowd the doorway, while inside you can take away big scoops of turmeric, cumin and fennel or order them freshly ground.

🏛 MUSTAFA CENTRE *Department Store*
☎ 6295 5855; 145 Syed Alwi Rd;
🕑 24hr; Ⓜ Farrer Park

A Singapore legend, as much cultural rite of passage as shopping experience, Mustafa's narrow aisles and tiny nooks have everything from electronics, clothing, toiletries, tacky clothes (lurid Bollywood shirts always make great presents), cheap DVDs, gold,

---

NANYANG ACADEMY OF FINE ARTS

For a peek at work being turned out by artists in Singapore and elsewhere in the region, stop by the various galleries located inside the **Nanyang Academy of Fine Arts** (☎ 6512 4071; 80 Bencoolen St; 🕑 11am-7pm Tue-Sun). Inside you'll find rotating exhibits including paintings, sculptures and other artworks by promising talents being unearthed in the new, creative Singapore.

---

moneychangers, a supermarket (it's the place to stock up on Indian spices and pickles) and sometimes half the population of Singapore.

🏛 PARCO BUGIS JUNCTION *Fashion*
☎ 6557 6557; 200 Victoria St; 11am-9pm; Ⓜ Bugis

More upscale than the Bugis St Market, this is a thicket of local streetwear outlets illustrating the revolving-door nature of Singapore fashion. Don't put off buying that T-shirt until tomorrow, because the shop may well have packed up and left by then.

🏛 SIM LIM SQUARE *IT, Mall*
☎ 6332 5839; 1 Rochor Canal Rd;
🕑 11am-9pm; Ⓜ Bugis

A byword for all that is cut-price and geeky, Sim Lim is not for those uninitiated in the world of sim cards, RAM, motherboards and soundcards. If you know what you're doing, there are real bargains to be had, but the untutored are more likely to be taken for a ride. Hard bargaining is essential.

◻ SUNGEI ROAD THIEVES MARKET *Street Market*
Sungei Rd, Weld Rd, Pasar Lane & Pitt St; 🕒 **10am-6pm;** Ⓜ **Little India, Bugis**
A true Singapore oddity, this collection of old geezers and dodgy characters splaying out random collections of used items on the pavement every day offers a peek into the underbelly of the city. Laptops, mobile phones, watches, DVDs, sneakers, boots and high-heeled shoes, rollerblades, battery chargers, an endless supply of power adapters and a variety of other electronic doo-dads were among the items we saw on our last visit. Everyone expects the authorities to close it down any day, but somehow it continues to thrive.

◻ TEKKA CENTRE *Textiles*
cnr Serangoon & Buffalo Rds; 🕒 **10am-9pm;** Ⓜ **Little India**
Once you've fought your way through the hawker centre and the rather lurid wet market (avoid it if you don't like severed sheep's heads), there's a whole floor of textile and sari shops on the 1st level – the cheapest place to pick

up an Indian outfit. Prices are labelled, but bargaining is expected.

🍴 EAT
It hardly needs saying: the sheer wealth of superb Indian food here is overwhelming. Though still dominated by the cuisines of the South, a recent influx of North Indian professionals has seen a new wave of Northern food hit the area. Down in the Arab Quarter, a renaissance in Middle Eastern eating is in full swing, while across Beach Rd, cheap Thai feasts await at the Golden Mile Complex.

🍴 ANANDA BHAVAN
Vegetarian $
☎ **6297 9522; Block 663, 01-10, Buffalo Rd;** 🕒 **6.30am-10.30pm;** Ⓜ **Little India;** ♿ Ⓥ 👶
This unassuming chain restaurant serves wonderful North and South Indian vegie fare, and at amazingly low prices. There are other Little India outlets on Serangoon Rd and Syed Alwi Rd, near Mustafa Centre, and even two 24-hour branches, one at 58 Serangoon Rd and the other at Changi Airport's Terminal 2.

🍴 ANDHRA CURRY *Indian* $$
☎ **6293 3935; 41 Kerbau Rd;** 🕒 **11.30am-3.30pm & 6-10.30pm Mon-Fri, 11.30am-10.30pm Sat & Sun;** Ⓜ **Little India;** ♿ 👶 Ⓥ

This no-frills, no-ceremony restaurant specialises in fiery recipes from the South Indian state of Andhra Pradesh. Attentive staff dish up Hyderabadi biryani (traditionally cooked in a dough-sealed pot), a very hot dry mutton curry and large vegetarian thalis. Packed on Sundays.

⑪ ANJAPPAR *Indian* $$
☎ 6392 5545; www.anjappar.com.sg;
102 Syed Alwi Rd; ⊗ 11.30am-11.30pm;
Ⓜ Farrer Park; ⃟ Ⓥ ♿

The two Little India outlets of this Chennai-based dynasty serve up

outstanding Chettinaad cuisine, from the deep south of India. Our favourites are the mutton *uppu kari* and the chicken *nattu koli masala*, the latter guaranteed to have you gasping in blissful chilli heaven. The flagship branch is on Race Course Rd, but the service is better here.

⑪ BANANA LEAF APOLO
Indian $$
☎ 6297 8682; 54-58 Race Course Rd;
⊗ 10.30am-10.30pm; Ⓜ Little India;
Ⓥ ♿

A popular stop on the tourist trail, but the uncompromisingly fiery

Visitors will find a stunning array of both fresh and cooked produce in Little India

NEIGHBOURHOODS

LITTLE INDIA & THE ARAB QUARTER

CHANDER ROAD
Tucked behind its more illustrious Race Course Rd neighbour and almost completely undiscovered by visitors, Chander Rd is also a treasure chest of Indian food – often at much lower prices. Have a wander and see what takes your fancy, but **Gandhi** (☎ 6299 5343; 31 Chander Rd), **Masala Hut** (☎ 6341 5101; 37 Chander Rd) and **Chettinadu** (☎ 6291 7161; 41 Chander Rd) all do a good trade.

food here has legions of fans both local and foreign, though the service can be poor. Offers a wide range of Indian food, all served up on banana leaves, but is most famous for its blistering fish-head curry. The branch in the Little India Arcade on 48 Serangoon Rd serves the same fare, and is equally good.

🍴 CAFÉ LE CAIRE
Middle Eastern $
☎ 6292 0979; 39-33 Arab St; 🕙 10am-5.30am; Ⓜ Bugis; ♿ Ⓥ ♨
Blink and you'll miss it during the day, but at night this alcohol-free Egyptian cafe becomes a miniature scene, especially at the weekend, colonising both sides of the street with its tables and rugs, filling with lounging *shisha*-smokers and eager diners gorging on the kebabs and superb dips. A must.

🍴 FRENCH STALL *French* $$
☎ 6299 3544; 544 Serangoon Rd; 🕙 drinks & coffee 3-6pm, meals 6-10pm; Ⓜ Farrer Park; ♿ ♨
Set up by two-Michelin-star chef Xavier Le Henaff to debunk the notion that French food is expensive, this unpretentious stall is a gem – great food, great desserts and great wine in a coffee-shop environment.

🍴 GOLDEN MILE COMPLEX
Thai $$
5001 Beach Rd; 🕙 11am-10.30pm; Ⓜ Bugis, Lavender
Singapore's Little Thailand. Forget all the fancy restaurants with their Buddha statues and cultural knick-knacks, if you want real Thai food, brave the stumbling drunken Isaan workers in this seedy old shopping centre for an evening of friendly service, cheap Singha and

TRIPPIES & CHILDREN'S LITTLE MUSEUM
The sort of place Pee Wee Herman might run, it's hard to categorize **Trippies** (☎ 9114 9686; 42 Bussorah St; 11am-9.30pm; Ⓜ Bugis). Is it a cafe? It *does* serve coffee and cake in the back. Is it a curios shop? You can find all sorts of interesting items downstairs. Is it a museum? It costs a dollar to go upstairs to see the big collection of memorabilia from the '50s, '60s and beyond. Why not visit and see for yourself?

sôm-tam (papaya salad). It's uniformly superb (the northeastern Thai food is best), but the Nong Khai Food & Beer Garden on the ground floor is particularly good. Complete the experience at Thai Disco 1 or 2 (see p94) afterwards.

RED PLACE'S BBQ Korean $$
☎ 6291 2588; 249 Beach Rd;
⏲ 11.30am-11pm; Ⓜ Bugis; ♿ ♿
An alternative to the area's ubiquitous Middle Eastern fare, this is always packed with Singaporean diners at night, feasting on kim chi (pickled cabbage), hotpot and other Korean classics.

SUNGEI RD LAKSA Laksa $
01-100, Jin Shui Kopitiam, Jalan Besar;
⏲ 9am-6pm; Ⓜ Lavender
Selected by the Makansutra street-food guru as Singapore's best laksa and who's to argue? Apparently this laksa master uses only charcoal to keep his precious gravy warm and, unlike other successful hawkers, refuses to open other branches. Get there around 11.30am or after 2pm to avoid the lunchtime rush.

TEKKA CENTRE
Hawker Centre $
cnr Serangoon & Buffalo Rds; ⏲ 7am-11pm; Ⓜ Little India; ♿ Ⓥ ♿
Queue up for biryani, dosai (South Indian savoury pancake), roti prata and teh tarik (pulled tea), then

SHOPPING FOR BODY & SPIRIT
Though you can buy all manner of spiritual knick-knacks throughout Singapore, the Albert/Waterloo Sts pedestrian mall may well be the nexus of religious-themed shopping, geomancy and fortune telling. Waterloo St (just by the Kuan Im Thong Hood Cho Temple) is home to several Chinese fortune tellers who'll prognosticate for about $10, and the famous Fu Lou Shou complex (on Albert St) is your one-stop shop for all things spiritual, from massive Buddha statues to smaller icons and religious ornamentation.

wedge yourself into a table at this legendary hawker centre wrapped around the sloshed guts and hacked bones of the wet market.

🍸 DRINK

🍸 BLUJAZ CAFÉ Pub
☎ 6292 3800; 11 Bali Lane; ⏲ noon-midnight Mon-Thu, noon-2am Fri, 4pm-2am Sat; Ⓜ Bugis; ♿
A beautiful old building, renovated as a bar and decorated in a decidedly eccentric bohemian style which, coupled with its location on the edge of the Arab Quarter and next to an artists' studio, makes it pretty much unique in Singapore. Live jazz downstairs on Monday, Friday and Saturday completes the mood.

☝ GOING OM
Cafe-Bar

☎ 6297 9197; 63 Haji Lane; 5pm-2am Sun-Thu, 5pm-4am Fri & Sat; Ⓜ Bugis

Part cafe, part chill-out space. The chilled-out seating area downstairs offers *shisha*, cocktails, coffees, teas and even 'chakra drinks' of seven colours (one for each chakra). Upstairs has a flexible space for yoga, tarot-card readings and group meditation. There's fire-spinning on Thursday nights, and even a house magician on Wednesdays. A unique find indeed.

☝ PRINCE OF WALES *Pub*

☎ 6299 0310; 101 Dunlop St; 🕐 9am-1am; Ⓜ Little India

Rough at the edges, knockabout Australian-style pub and beer garden, with scuffed wooden floors, Gippsland Pale on tap, acoustic strummers and live bands, and appropriately laconic blokes behind the bar. A slightly surreal enclave of non-Indians amid the Sunday evening Little India melee.

☝ THAI DISCO *Nightclub*

☎ 6295 1611; 02-85, Golden Mile Complex, 5001 Beach Rd; 🕐 8pm-3am Mon-Fri, 8pm-4am Sat, 6pm-3am Sun; Ⓜ Lavender

Thoroughly raucous, slightly seedy and heartily drunken – it's a Thai

disco! The house band, featuring scantily dressed female singers and heavily hair-gelled male heart-throbs, play danceable rock classics at high volume, while admirers buy garlands to place around their necks. You're likely to be the only tourist in here, but no one seems to care.

⭐ PLAY

☆ CLIMB ASIA *Climbing*

☎ 6292 7701; www.climb-asia.com; 60 Tessensohn Rd; admission before/after 5pm $6/8, membership $40; 🕐 5-11pm Mon, noon-11pm Tue-Fri, 10am-9pm Sat & Sun

Highly professional climb centre with a challenging series of indoor walls, a realistic outdoor wall and a boulder cave. Good spot to get the lowdown on climbing spots around the region.

☆ REX THEATRE *Movie Theatre*

☎ 6337 0025; 2 Mackenzie Rd; tickets $10; 🕐 noon-midnight Sun-Thu, noon-3am Fri & Sat; Ⓜ Little India

Where can you go to see the Bollywood blockbusters advertised on posters in restaurants all over Little India? Why, at the Rex, of course. This beautifully renovated historic three-screen theatre shows films from around the subcontinent, most subtitled in English.

Jonathan Atherton
Singapore-based stand-up comic

Funniest Singlish word or phrase? 'La', because it means everything. And nothing… **Why did the chicken cross Orchard Rd?** I don't know, but when you find out how she did it, please let me know. I'm still stuck in a maze under Ion shopping centre. **How many Singaporeans does it take to screw in a light bulb?** None. That's the maid's job. **What's the funniest Singapore scene you've ever witnessed?** I was taking my friend Chris McCausland, a blind British comic, on a guided tour of Geylang. My wife and his girlfriend were with us. A lady of the evening passed us by, strutting her stuff. Chris, being blind, stared straight ahead. She turned to me and asked 'Is your friend a snob?' 'No,' I replied, 'he's blind.' She took his hands and placed them on her breasts. My wife asked his girlfriend 'Are you OK with that?' 'It's alright,' she replied, 'he's only looking.' **What's the best place in town for a laugh?** Any car park. But if you want to see something intentionally funny, you should check out what's happening in town at www.thecomedyclub.asia.

>SENTOSA

Not long ago Singapore's self-styled pleasure isle was a national joke, its attractions either ageing and fading or depressing, deserted flops, lampooned by locals, tourists and guidebooks as feeble and kitsch.

Those days are well behind Sentosa now, but how you feel about the place depends largely on your own tastes. Two long-anticipated projects opened in 2010: the vast Resorts World Sentosa Casino (bringing a touch of Las Vegas to the once stodgy island state) and the Universal Studios Theme Park. Sentosa also boasts top-notch hotels, two world-class golf courses, excellent restaurants, two luge tracks, a Segway tour, a restaurant with a built-in wave pool, trendy beach bars with dance parties and even beaches that are, by Singapore standards, none too shabby. These elements bring hordes of young Singaporeans onto the island day and night, and the developers have bet big bucks that Sentosa will be known internationally in the years to come.

Thoroughly artificial though it is, Sentosa is national joke no longer. It's not only cool to admit you came here, it's even OK to tell people you had a good time.

SENTOSA

👁 SEE
Cineblast &
  4D Magix **1** B2
Dolphin Lagoon **2** C3
Fort Siloso **3** A1
Images of
  Singapore **4** B2
Songs of the Sea **5** B2
Underwater World **6** A2

🍴 EAT
Coastes 7 B2
Samundar 8 C3
Suburbia 9 C3
The Cliff 10 C3
Wave House ....(see 13)

⭐ PLAY
Sentosa Golf Club 14 D3
Sentosa Luge 15 B2
Sentosa Segway
  Eco Adventure 16 B2
Sentosa Skyride 17 B2
The Flying Trapeze 18 A2
Universal Studios
  Singapore 19 C2
Wave House ....(see 13)

🍸 DRINK
Azzura Beach Club **11** B2
Café del Mar **12** B2
Wave House **13** B2

GETTING THERE & AROUND

Aside from getting a taxi straight across – the fastest, though most expensive option – there are several dedicated methods of crossing the harbour. Once on the island, a series of colour-coded bus services and a beach tram – routes for which are laid out on the free visitors map – shuttle people around the island. Many city buses run to the HarbourFront exchange where you can catch the Sentosa bus.

> **Sentosa Bus** ($2; ⏱ 7am-11pm Sun-Thu, 7am-midnight Fri & Sat) Runs between HarbourFront bus interchange and the Beach Station. Buy tickets at HarbourFront.

> **Sentosa Express Monorail** ($3, includes entry fee to Sentosa; ⏱ 7am-midnight) Board at Vivocity Shopping Centre.

> **SIA Hop-On** (www.singaporeair.com/hop-on; adult/child $12/6, SIA passengers $3) Stops at major shopping malls and hotels in the city.

◉ SEE

Sentosa can keep you occupied for a couple of days, though a single day is usually enough for most. Universal Studios and the Integrated Resort is operated by Resorts World Sentosa (☎ 6577 8888; www.rwsentosa.com). Other attractions are operated under the Sentosa management umbrella and information on any of them can be obtained from the island hotline or website (☎ 1800 736 8672; www.sentosa.com.sg).

◉ CINEBLAST & 4D MAGIX
adult/child (either venue) $18/11, combo package $29.90/17.90; ⏱ **10am-9pm**
Cineblast is a simulation ride that simulates a variety of high-speed experiences, and 4D Magix is a state-of-the-art theatre offering the latest in movie magic. Children

should especially enjoy both experiences.

◉ FORT SILOSO
adult/child $8/5; ⏱ **10am-6pm;** ♿
Preserved British coastal fort that proved famously useless when the Japanese stormed Singapore from the north in WWII. Documentaries, artefacts, animatronics and re-created historical scenes will absorb history buffs, while their kids tug them towards the exits.

◉ IMAGES OF SINGAPORE
adult/child $10/7; ⏱ **9am-7pm;** ♿
Thoroughly reworked interactive panorama of the island's history, going back to the 14th century and featuring re-creations and the ubiquitous life-size models Singapore's attractions love so dearly. Despite some inevitable political

Authentic re-creation of an old army barracks at Fort Siloso

spin and tacky merchandising, it's enjoyable.

SONGS OF THE SEA
adult/child $10; 🕐 **shows 7.40pm & 8.40pm;** ♿
Extravagant light and-sound show set around a replica Malay fisherman's village. The location and the visual effects are stun-

ning but the Lloyd Webber–esque theatricality veers towards the cheesy.

UNDERWATER WORLD & DOLPHIN LAGOON
adult/child $19.90/12.70; 🕐 **9am-9pm;** ♿
Ageing slightly, and set to be completely eclipsed by the

world's largest oceanarium at the island's new casino resort, children will nonetheless get a kick out of the giant spider crabs, sting rays and impossibly lovable manatee. Tickets include entry to the Dolphin Lagoon show further along the coast.

EAT

When it came to food options, Sentosa Island used to be a saturated fat–laden hell of junk-food outlets and stalls selling bad, overpriced versions of Singapore hawker staples. How things change. There is now good food to be found pretty much everywhere and among the medals Sentosa likes to pin on its chest are a couple of the city's best restaurants.

🍽 COASTES
European $$

☎ 6274 9668; Siloso Beach; 🕒 10am-10pm Mon-Thu, 11am-1am Fri & Sat, 9am-10pm Sun; 🚻 ♿

Coastes is the best of the Sentosa beach eateries, serving up excellent pizzas, pasta and curries to a relaxed crowd. Grab a rustic table under the pergola, or look louche on the sun loungers. It's not exclusively for the hip, tanned and beautiful, as the thumping music suggests.

🍽 SAMUNDAR
Indian $$

☎ 6276 8891; www.samundar.com.sg; 85 Palawan Beach Walk; 🕒 10.30am-10pm Mon-Thu, 10.30am-11pm Fri-Sun; ♿ Ⓥ 🚻

Avoid the air-con inside and grab an outdoor table, a few beers and order up big from the tandoor menu at this beachside beauty. The North Indian bias suggests it's aimed squarely at the legions of Indian tourists on Sentosa. Features an extensive vegetarian menu.

🍽 SUBURBIA
Wine Bar $$

☎ 6376 5938; www.suburbia.com.sg; 🕒 3-10pm Mon-Thu, 3-10.30pm Fri & Sat; ♿

This is a cool, modern wine bar and restaurant in a lush garden setting. Sure, it doesn't have the sea views of other Sentosa competitors, and the building looks a bit like a university science block, but at night it's a perfect spot to sit outside and down a bottle or two.

🍽 THE CLIFF
Seafood $$$

☎ 6275 0331; www.thesentosa.com; 2 Bukit Manis Rd; 🕒 6.30-11pm (last orders 9.30pm); ♿

With its stunning views, a breezy clifftop outdoor setting and a superb seafood selection, this res-

STAYING ON SENTOSA

Bali it ain't, but waking up on Sentosa can still put you in the holiday mood. The **Sentosa** (☎ 6275 0331; www.thesentosa.com) has fabulous rooms and junior suites, and the **Amara Sanctuary** (☎ 6825 3888; www.amarasanctuary.com) offers private villas that come with private plunge pools and outdoor baths. Of course, the newest and flashiest game in town has got to be the properties managed by the **Integrated Resort/Universal Studios** (☎ 1800 736 8672; www.sentosa.com.sg) including the **Hotel Michael**, which looks something like a cruise ship from the outside, and the ultra-exclusive (invitation only, in fact) **Crockford Towers**. In 2011 there will be six hotels in total managed by the group. Two Sentosa stalwarts, the **Costa Sands Resort** (☎ 6275 1034; www.costasands.com.sg) and the **Siloso Beach Resort** (☎ 6722 3333; www.silosobeachresort.com), are also good choices.

taurant rivals Il Lido for romance. Make the experience even better by choosing to retire to one of the hotel's junior suites after dinner. With all those oysters around, you might need it. Definitely one of Singapore's best spots to eat.

▶ DRINK

Sentosa has made a conscious effort to generate a cool edge to its image to attract the city's affluent, fashionable youth. Beach raves have been a wild success, though there has been talk of stopping them, and the beachfront Balearic-style clubs attract legions of the tanned.

▶ AZZURA BEACH CLUB
Bar, Bistro

☎ 6270 8003; 10am-10.30pm Mon-Fri, 10am-6am Sat & Sun;

Singapore has never been thought of as a 'beach bar' kind of place, but all that may change once folks get wind of this new and incredibly hip (so hip it almost hurts) bar and bistro located right on the Sentosa sands.

▶ CAFÉ DEL MAR
Bar, Nightclub

☎ 6235 1296; www.cafedelmar.com.sg; 40 Siloso Beach Walk; 11am-1am Mon-Thu, 11am-4am Fri, 10am-4am Sat, 10am-1am Sun;

Café del Mar evidently objects to the idea of a quiet day at the beach, but at night after the deafened day-trippers in the vicinity have crept home this Ibiza-inspired bar comes into its own. Day beds and pastel pouffes on the sand, a poolside bar, Saturday bikini foam parties, DJs...you get the picture.

WAVE HOUSE
Bar, Restaurant, Surf Park

☎ 6377 3113; wavehousesentosa.com; 10am-midnight Sun-Thu, 10am-2am Fri & Sat; 🚻 ♿ Ⓥ

Is it a bar? A restaurant? Or a surf park? Why, all three: a first-class restaurant serving excellent continental and Asian cuisine, and an excellent bar that just happens to have two wave pools on the premises. It rents surf equipment, so after your pasta primavera or strawberry daiquiri you can grab a board and ride the artificial rip curl.

You can expect plenty of sun, sea, booze and bikinis at Café del Mar (p101)

⭐ PLAY

⭐ SENTOSA GOLF CLUB *Golf*

☎ 6275 0090; www.sentosagolf
.com; Bukit Manis Rd; Tanjong course
weekday/weekend $280/400, Serapong
course $310/450; ⏲ tee-off sessions
7.35-9.20am & 12.45-2.25pm

Boasting two lush, immaculate
championship-level courses,
Sentosa has successfully pitched
(pardon the pun) itself as one of
the island's most prestigious clubs.
Book well in advance.

⭐ SENTOSA LUGE & SKYRIDE *Luge*

1/2/3/5 rides $12/17/21/29;
⏲ 10am-9.30pm

Imported from New Zealand, so
you know it must involve some
adventurousness, the luge is an
irresistible 60 seconds of racing
family and friends through hairpin
bends and bone-shaking straights
carved through the forest. The
newly added second track is
steeper, longer and even more
hair-raising (helmets are provided
and mandatory!).

⭐ SENTOSA SEGWAY ECO ADVENTURE *Tour*

☎ 9825 4066; www.segway-sentosa.
com; fun ride $12, eco adventure $38;
⏲ 10am-9.30pm; ♿

Segway gives visitors the
opportunity to ride around
Sentosa. Though high on the
geek factor, the rides are plenty
of fun. $12 gets you a ride around
a track, while $38 gets you a full
tour – with guide – around the
island.

⭐ THE FLYING TRAPEZE *Trapeze*

Trapeze School; per swing $10, three swings
$20; ⏲ 4-6pm Tue-Fri, 4-7pm Sat & Sun

Do kids still dream of running
away to the circus? Perhaps the
lure of mounting the trapeze still
runs deep – deeper hopefully
than the desire to wear a lycra
bodysuit.

⭐ UNIVERSAL STUDIOS SINGAPORE *Theme Park*

☎ 6577 8899; www.rwsentosa.com;
adult/child Mon-Fri $66/48, Sat & Sun
$72/52; ⏲ 9am-6pm; ♿ ♿

Universal Studios (part of the
massive Resorts World Singapore)
has everything you'd expect
from a Hollywood-style theme
park plunked down (at great
expense) in Southeast Asia.
Rides, attractions and a constant
soundtrack of dramatic music will
make you feel like you're trapped
in a big-budget Hollywood action
film all day long.

>EASTERN SINGAPORE

Boasting some of Singapore's oldest neighbourhoods and best restaurants, Singapore's eastern end is gaining in popularity among both travellers and long-term expatriates.

The twin historical districts of Geylang and Katong (both traditionally Malay quarters) have very different characteristics. Geylang offers a serious cultural juxtaposition, being at once the notorious centre of Singapore's red-light district (featuring prostitutes, legalised brothels and illegal back-alley gambling) and home to streets filled with shrines, temples and other religious organisations. To throw cuisine into the mix, many locals say Geylang has the best local food.

Further east, Katong (also known as Joo Chiat) is the centre of Singapore's Peranakan community, whose ornate shophouses line the area around Joo Chiat Rd, another excellent hunting ground for food.

Lining the shore is the large East Coast Park, an urban seaside oasis boasting bicycling and skating paths, decent windsurfing beaches, great restaurants, hawker centres and bars, and even a brand new skateboard park.

EASTERN SINGAPORE

⊙ SEE

⊙ CHANGI MEMORIAL & CHAPEL

☎ 6214 2451; www.changimuseum.com;
1000 Upper Changi Rd North; admission
free; ⊙ 9.30am-5pm; Ⓜ Tanah Merah,
then bus 2

The destruction of the original site
to make way for prison expansion
was an affront to many POWs
who suffered terribly at the hands
of the Japanese, but give some
credit to the authorities for moving the memorial elsewhere. The
photographs, letters and drawings
graphically illustrate the horror
of WWII and the chapel itself is
a moving re-creation of the kind
built by the prisoners from the
period.

⊙ KATONG ANTIQUES HOUSE

☎ 6345 8544; 208 East Coast Rd;
⊙ 11am-6.30pm (call for appointment);
🚌 10, 14

A rare opportunity to see a
preserved Peranakan house, filled
with original or carefully restored
antiques, from jewellery to furniture and, of course, beadwork. The
owner is a true enthusiast.

⊞ EAT

Welcome to the heartland of
Singapore cuisine. The dazzling
development that has swamped
much of Singapore has bypassed
most of Geylang and Katong,
where rough-and-ready hawker
centres and coffee shops dominate. East Coast Park is less intimidating, with its popular outdoor
seafront 'food village' and famous
seafood centre.

⊞ 328 KATONG LAKSA

Hawker Stall $

☎ 9732 8163; 216 East Coast Rd;
⊙ 8.30am-9pm; Ⓜ Eunos, then walk;
🚌 10, 12, 14, 32; ♿

One day maybe someone will
unearth an ancient scroll describing the original Katong laksa, and
the unending dispute between the
neighbouring stalls here over who
was first will finally end. Until then,
you won't go wrong with the rich
and creamy offering here. Was it
first? Do we care? The expanding
size and opening of new branches
would suggest it's the most popular, or at least the most business-
savvy.

A STROLL ALONG THE BEACH

If Beach Rd sounds like a strange name
for a road several hundred metres from
the sea, it really isn't. Not so long ago,
every inch of land beyond it didn't exist.
In fact, the country used to be a staggering 135 sq km smaller – and there
are plans for another 100 sq km of expansion in the future via further land
reclamation.

¶¶ CHILLI PADI *Peranakan* $$

☎ 6275 1002; 11 Joo Chiat Pl;
🕑 11am-2.30pm, 5.30-10pm;
Ⓜ Eunos, then walk; 🚶

Homestyle Nonya cooking, set in a row of picturesque shophouses in the heart of Peranakan country. Dig into some fiery, sour *asam* (tamarind) fish head, the range of classic chicken dishes, or the *sambal* (spicy shrimp paste) seafood. Its success has spawned other branches and a range of home-cook pastes.

¶¶ DUNMAN ROAD FOOD CENTRE *Hawker Centre* $

Cnr Joo Chiat Rd & Dunman Rd;
🕑 8am-10pm; Ⓜ Paya Lebar, then walk or taxi; 🚶

Though all of the vendors here serve wonderful food, the near-constant queue-up for food at Ah Eng's Wonton Noodles on the lower level speaks volumes. In the stall next door, Ken's Delights keeps the *cendol* and dessert crowds coming back for more.

¶¶ EAST COAST LAGOON FOOD VILLAGE *Hawker Centre* $

East Coast Park Service Rd; 🕑 10.30am-11pm; Ⓜ Bedok, then taxi, 🚌 401 from Bedok MRT (weekends only); 🚶 🚶

Certainly there can be few hawker centres with a better location. Tramp barefoot off the beach, order up some *satay* (meat skewers cooked over a flame), seafood,

GETTING THERE & AROUND

> MRT - The East West Line runs along the fringe of East Coast. The new Circle Line now stops at Paya Lebar and Dakota.
> Bus - 2, 13, 21, 26 run along Sims Ave through Geylang. 10 and 14 run along East Coast Rd and Upper East Coast Rd, while 15, 31 and 76 service Marine Parade Rd.

or the uniquely Singaporean *satay bee hoon* (rice vermicelli) from Meng Kee at stall 17 (get there before 6pm, or you'll end up in a long queue).

¶¶ ENG SENG *Hawker Centre* $

☎ 6440 5560; 247/249 Joo Chiat Pl;
🕑 5pm-9pm; Ⓜ Eunos, then bus 155;
🚶 🚶

Known all over the island for its black-pepper crab (though – surprise, surprise – many dispute its pre-eminence) the queues start before 5pm. People duck out of work early to eat here. The crab is worth the wait, but if you're hungry and impatient the barbecue seafood stall also has several loyal fans.

¶¶ GUAN HOE SOON *Peranakan* $$

☎ 6344 2761; 38/40 Joo Chiat Pl;
🕑 11am-2.30pm & 6-9.30pm Wed-Mon;
Ⓜ Eunos, then bus 155; 🚶

FOOD WARS

In a country as opinionated about food as Singapore, it's not surprising that regular wars break out between hawkers claiming to be the best, the original, the most famous, the only...some disputes have even ended in legal action. The most renowned was over Katong Laksa – dubbed by the media as the unresolved 'laksa wars', after which 328 Katong Laksa, Original Katong Laksa (also known as Marine Parade Laksa) and the somewhat adamantly named Janggut the Original Katong Laksa Since 1950 were all still standing.

New location, same famous chef. The food at this heritage restaurant (one of Lee Kuan Yew's favourites) is absolutely superb. Try the *sotong sambal* (squid in *sambal*) or, our favourite Peranakan dish, *ayam buah keluak* (chicken cooked with black nut). Save room for the desert, *chendool* (spelled a bit differently than its Malay counterpart), an absolutely fantastic iced treat that may well make your eyes roll back in your skull in pleasure.

🍽 JUST GREENS VEGETARIAN
Vegetarian $

☎ 6345 0069; 49/51 Joo Chiat Pl; ⏰ 8am-10pm; Ⓜ Eunos, then taxi or walk; ♿ Ⓥ

You know the vegetarian food must be good when you're lined up alongside Buddhist monks (queuing for food is a good sign). Pick from the menu in the dining room, or choose from the selections at the door and take them inside.

🍽 MANGO TREE *Indian* $$

☎ 6442 8655; 1000 East Coast Parkway; ⏰ noon-2.30pm & 6.30-10.30pm Mon-Fri, 11.30am-midnight Sat, Sun & holidays; Ⓜ Eunos, then taxi, 🚌 401 from Bedok MRT (weekends only)

Tiny, elegant, cosy beachfront restaurant specialising in food from Kerala and Goa. The best spot is outside on the small deck, where you can catch the breeze, though the atmosphere is mildly spoiled by the bars sandwiching it either side.

🍽 NO SIGNBOARD SEAFOOD
Seafood $$

☎ 6842 3415; 414 Geylang Rd; ⏰ noon-2am; Ⓜ Aljunied; ♿ 🚻

Legends of hawkers-turned-millionaires abound in Singapore, and few are more irresistible than that of No Signboard Seafood. The fame of the white-pepper crab here has helped spawn five branches around the city, but this is the original restaurant – and it stays open later than the other branches, which are at East Coast Seafood Centre, Katong, Vivocity and the Esplanade.

Tony Tan
Hostel owner, tour guide – Betel Box (p194)

Best place to bring an out-of-towner to shatter their expectations about Singapore? Geylang (p104) feeds the senses like nowhere else in Singapore. The pungent scent of durian, the sound of prayer from the many places of worship, and even the flutter of neon lights from the houses of ill repute. **Good place to bring kids?** The Science Centre Singapore (p140) is really good for families. Do look out for the visiting exhibitions there and make time for at least one IMAX film! Even at my age, I still spend way too much time in their toy shop. **Best place to spend a rainy day?** The Bras Basah Complex. Locals call it 'Book City' because it has the highest concentration of independent book retailers and secondhand bookstores in a single building. My favourite shop is Basheer Graphic Books (p87) on the 4th floor. **What keeps you in Joo Chiat?** The community, the food, the architecture and the beach. No other part of Singapore even comes close to keeping me excited and involved. In Singapore, many believe that once you are an East Coaster, you will never want to live anywhere else.

🍴 OLD AIRPORT ROAD FOOD CENTRE *Hawker Centre* $

Block 51, Old Airport Rd; 🕙 **10am-late;** Ⓜ **Dakota;** ♿ Ⓥ 🚻

A long-time favourite (now easier to get to thanks to the new Circle line), this hawker centre is home to beloved stalls such as Matter Rd Seafood (famous for white-pepper crab) and Toah Payoh Rojah. Feel like lighter fare? Check out the herbal offerings at House of Soup.

🍴 SIN HUAT SEAFOOD RESTAURANT *Seafood* $$$

☎ **6744 9755; Lorong 35, Geylang Rd;** 🕙 **11am-late;** Ⓜ **Aljunied, then walk;** ♿

Perhaps the most famous seafood joint in Singapore – and certainly the priciest hawker food. Chef Danny Lim is renowned for his crab *bee hoon* (rice noodles), yet Sin Huat is determinedly grungy and its fame has inspired some desultory, if not rude, service. They know people will keep flocking in, so they're not too bothered. If you want to eat sooner rather than later, try something else, such as the *gong gong* (whelks) or 'MRT' prawns.

🍴 THE GARDEN SLUG *Eclectic* $

☎ **6346 0504; www.thegardenslug.com; 55 Lorong L Teok Kurau, 01-59/61 Bright Centre;** 🕙 **6-10pm Mon & Tue, 10am-10pm Wed & Thu, 9am-10pm Fri-Sun;** Ⓜ **Eunos then walk/bus 155;** ♿ Ⓥ 🚻

Fancy a soothing alternative to chilli crab and Peranakan cuisine?

COOKING UP A STORM

If you learn how to cook Singapore-style, you won't need to come back! Classes run from two to four hours; some are hands-on, some are instruction only. Call for bookings and schedules.

> **at-sunrice GlobalChef Academy** (Map pp68-9; ☎ 6336 3307; www.at-sunrice.com; Fort Canning Centre, Fort Canning Park; classes $35-135; Ⓜ Dhoby Ghaut) Half-day classes with a spicy hands-on emphasis.

> **Cookery Magic** (Map p105; ☎ 6348 9667; www.cookerymagic.com; Haig Rd, Katong; classes $60; Ⓜ Paya Lebar) Offering home-based Asian cooking classes in a colonial home with an enchanting and beautiful tropical garden. Weekday classes are held from 10.30am to 1.30pm or 3pm to 6pm. Chef Ruqxana also occasionally holds classes on Pulau Ubin.

> **Coriander Leaf** (Map pp68-9; ☎ 6732 3354; www.corianderleaf.com; 02-03, 3A Merchant Court, River Valley Rd; classes from $130; Ⓜ Clarke Quay) Pan-Asian and Euro delights for small groups. See also p74.

> **Shermay's Cooking School** (Map pp118-9; ☎ 6479 8442; www.shermay.com; 01-76 Block 43, Jln Merah Saga, Chip Bee Gardens, Holland Village; classes $69-139; 🚌 7, 61, 77) Singaporean, Peranakan and chocolate are Shermay's faves!

SAILING ON

Though Singapore may not have Asia's nicest beaches (hard to be that and the region's busiest shipping hub simultaneously), the East Coast is quickly becoming known as a great spot for sailing and windsurfing, thanks to a combination of OK beaches and year-round wind. One new spot catering to the wind-warrior set is **Constant Wind** (☎ 6445 5108; www.constantwind.com; 11 Changi Coast Way; 10.30am-6pm), which rents windsurfing and sailing gear. Constant Wind also teaches four-hour courses in windsurfing for $66, as well as offering sailing courses and coaching. Its stretch of beach is under Changi Airport's flight path, so sailors are guaranteed regular bursts of intense wind.

The Garden Slug serves somewhat mellower cuisine, including homemade soups, salads and beautiful all-day breakfasts (try the pancakes!) in an absolutely chilled-out spot on a suburban side-street.

☷ VANSH *Indian* $$
☎ 6345 4466; 2 Stadium Walk; noon-2.30pm & 6-11pm; Ⓜ Kallang, then taxi; Ⓥ ♿

An unusual Indian restaurant, in that it's ditched the usual Indian decor in favour of an eye-catching modern design with recessed, cushion-laden seating, Vansh's take on the cuisine is equally impressive. The tandoor offerings

are superb – or go on Sundays for all-you-can-eat kebabs and beer.

☷ YONG HE EATING HOUSE
Hawker Centre $
☎ 6745 5682; Lorong 27 Geylang Rd; 24hr; Ⓜ Aljunied, then walk; Ⓥ

Despite the fear of being spotted in Geylang at night, people flock to this all-night joint for its famous hot soya-bean milk, sweet bean-curd desserts and pork floss, though it's a bit too close to the sleaze for some.

🍸 DRINK

🍸 BARK CAFÉ *Cafe, Bar*
☎ 6545 4118; 1000 Upper Changi Rd Nth; noon-12.30am Mon-Thu, to 1.30am Fri-Sun; Ⓜ Tanah Merah, then bus 2; ♿

A relaxed, easygoing cafe right next door to the Changi Chapel, the Bark stays fairly low-key even on weekend nights, with a friendly crowd of mainly local residents enjoying the outdoor breeze, pool table, ample beers and excellent local (and international) food. The 'red plum soda' is evidently of some repute.

🍸 BERNIE'S BFD *Pub*
☎ 6244 4434; 1000 East Coast Parkway; 5pm-midnight Mon-Fri, noon-midnight Sat & Sun; Ⓜ Eunos, then taxi, ☒ 401 from Bedok MRT (weekends only); ♿

Saloon bar popular with expats, taking full advantage of the sea breezes and its seaside location, but retaining the dimly lit, dark-wood interior serious boozers require. There's live music most nights.

Y CHARLIE'S CORNER *Pub*
☎ 6542 0867; 01-08, Changi Village Hawker Centre, 2 Changi Village Rd; ⏱ 11am-2.30pm & 6-11pm Mon-Sat; Ⓜ Tanah Merah, then bus 2; ♿

Absorbing the languid Changi Village vibe, Charlie's has been around forever, dishing up Western food to the residents in this hidden corner of the island. The food isn't fantastic, but the huge range of beers can detain you for hours. Pop in after a visit to Pulau Ubin (see boxed text, p114).

Y SUNSET BAY *Bar, Bistro*
☎ 6448 9060; 1300 East Coast Park; ⏱ 3pm-midnight Mon-Thu, 3pm-2am Fri, noon-2am Sat, noon-midnight Sun; 🚌 12, 13, 16; Ⓟ ♿

When the sun goes down you couldn't pick a more relaxed space to sit and watch the boats go by than this lovely seaside bar and bistro located in a quiet stretch of East Coast Park. The kitchen serves excellent Western and Asian dishes.

☆ PLAY

☆ GALLOP STABLE *Horse Riding*
☎ 6583 9665; 61 Pasir Ris Green; rides $10-60; ⏱ 8-11am & 2-7pm Tue-Sun; Ⓜ Pasir Ris; ♿

One for the kids – stables and a paddock surrounded by trees in Pasir Ris Park. Where the nippers can take an 800m ride led by a trainer or, if they know how to ride, take a canter themselves for $40 to $60. Parents can watch proudly from the cafe, or take part themselves. There are facilities for disabled riders, but call ahead.

☆ PASIR RIS PARK *Park*
Pasir Ris Dr 3; ⏱ 24hr; Ⓜ Pasir Ris

Heartlands Singapore is not all housing estates and hawker centres. You'll see few tourists in this superb seafront park, complete with a maze park, playgrounds,

---

RIDING THE COAST ROAD

One of the most pleasurable ways to pass a weekday afternoon (don't do this at weekends) is to cycle the length of East Coast Park. Pick up a bike at the Marine Cove rental station, go west past the surprisingly thick woods to the beginning of the path, then do a U-turn and head for Changi. The cycle path winds through gardens, nature reserves, restaurant strips, the Ski 360° lagoon, the East Coast Lagoon Food Village, Bedok jetty (check the little fisherman's camp next to it), past the PA Sea Sports Centre, then over a canal and past a quiet beach, where you can sit and watch the jets roaring right overhead as they come in to land at Changi Airport.

NEIGHBOURHOODS

EASTERN SINGAPORE

Fancy sliding down a three-storey-high half-pipe at the Wild Wild Wet theme park?

fishing pond, bike, rollerblade and kayak rental, horse riding (see left) and a pristine 5-hectare mangrove reserve ringed with boardwalks and birdwatcher's aerie. Of course, there are also eating options. Combine with Wild Wild Wet (right) for a family day out with a difference.

★ SKI 360° Cable Ski

☎ 6442 7318; www.ski360degree .com; 1206A East Coast Parkway; per hr weekdays/weekends $32/42; ⏲ 10am-10pm Mon-Thu, 10am-midnight Fri, 9am-midnight Sat, 9am-10pm Sun; Ⓜ Bedok, then bus 401 (weekends only), 🚌 196, 197

What better way to cool off than to strap on some water skis, a kneeboard or a wakeboard and get dragged around a lagoon on the end of a cable? OK, you could just go swimming, but where's the fun in that? Best visited on weekday mornings, when there's usu-

ally hardly anyone there – unless a school party happens to drop by. Also teaches wakeboarding; check the website for schedule.

★ WILD WILD WET Theme Park

☎ 6581 9135; www.wildwildwet.com; adult/child/family $15.50/10.80/42; ⏲ 1-7pm Mon & Wed-Fri, 10am-8pm Sat, Sun & school holidays; Ⓜ Pasir Ris

Part of the mushrooming Downtown East leisure complex, this water park doesn't boast the spectacular slides of its international rivals, but it's still lots of fun. Highlight is the unnerving Slide-Up, a three-storey-high half-pipe. Weekdays are best, unless it's a school holiday. At weekends you can combine Wild Wild Wet with a visit to the **Escape Theme Park** (☎ 6581 9112; www.escapethemepark.com; adult/child/ family $17.70/8.90/42.80), though the ageing rides will not impress kids accustomed to a diet of Disneyland and similar extravagances.

WORTH THE TRIP

Pulau Ubin (Map p115) is the Singapore that development left behind – a languid, ram-shackle island of few people and fewer cars, small villages, forests, fish farms, quiet country lanes, old quarries and plantations.

More akin to rural Malaysia than Singapore (if you have a mobile phone, you'll even get a message welcoming you to Malaysia), locals pour over here at weekends, filling the belching old bumboats that chug across the channel ($2.50 each way; operates 6am to 8pm) from Changi Point Ferry Terminal to the island jetty, to ride bikes along the narrow lanes and dirt tracks, dodging scurrying monitors, wild boar and sunbathing snakes.

Weekdays is the best time, when you'll have the island virtually to yourself. Docking at the jetty, where men fish from rocks and skeletal pilings jut from the water, is like entering another country. If you've come by taxi from downtown Singapore, it's quite a jolt – the pace suddenly shifts down into first gear, or even neutral.

Turn right at the end of the jetty to a small information kiosk, detailing Ubin's fauna and offering nuggets of history. Left from the jetty is the tiny village, where you can hire a mountain bike for between $2 and $15. Make sure you give the bikes a thorough check as the lower-end ones tend to be in poor condition. The village is also where you'll likely want to stock up on water, though there are shops selling snacks and water around the island.

West of the village you'll pass the Pekan Quarry, fenced off to deter explorers. Keep heading west and you'll cross a bridge over a tidal inlet and pass the Ubin Quarry. Resist the urge to swim or risk a fine of $1000.

Further on, the road forks. Right leads to the northern shore. Left leads to the strange **German Girl Shrine**, housed in a yellow hut under a tree to the left, where some Chinese devotees come to pray to the spirit of a young German who died there during WWI. This is also where you'll find the **Ketam Mountain Bike Park**. (Er, you did spend those extra few bucks for a quality bike, didn't you?)

At the extreme east of the island lies perhaps its most popular attraction, **Tanjong Chek Jawa**, a pristine mangrove threaded with boardwalks and a five-storey-high **observation tower**. It's often crowded on the weekends, but the area is nonetheless worth visiting at anytime.

Back in the village, reward yourself with a seafood feast and beers at **Season Live Seafood** next to the stony beach, or **Sin Lam Huat**, around the town square, for kampong dishes.

Among the places to stay the night on Ubin is the **Celestial Resort** (☎ 6542 6681; www.celestialresort.com; d from $98). Camping on **Noordin Beach** is also a nice way to go, especially as it's free.

To get to Changi Village (which has a superb hawker centre, almost worth the trip itself) take a taxi from the city (at least $20) or take Bus 2 or 29 from Tanah Merah MRT station.

MALAYSIA

800 m
0.4 miles

Strait of Johor

Sungai
Besar

Nuordin
Beach

Sungai
Memam

Mamam
Beach
Campite

Mamam Beach

Jl Noordin

Jl Mamam

Balai
Quarry

Ketam
Quarry

German Girl
Shrine

Sungai Puaka

Wei-Siam

Fish
Farm

Jl Sam Heng

Intertidal
Flats

Ketam
Mountain
Bike Park

Wei-Too Fa
Gong Temple

PULAU
UBIN

Jl Durian

Jl Ubin

Old Scottish
Cottage

Celestial
Resort

Ubin
Quarry

Jl Endut Senin

Jl Batu
Ubin

Jl Jelutong

Ubin First Stop Restaurant &
Sin Lam Huat

Pulau
Sekudu

Tanjong
Chek
Jawa

Pulau
Ketam

Ketam Channel

Sungai Jelutong

Pekan
Quarry

Ubin Police Post
Information Kiosk
Bicycle Rental Shops

Season
Live Seafood

Green
Hub @
Pulau Ubin

Serangoon
Harbour

Pulau
Ubin Ferry
Terminal

Strait of Johor

Changi
Point

Changi Village

Changi
Coast Rd

Loyang Rd

CHANGI

Pasir
Ris Park

Changi
Airport

Tampines
Xpwy

Pasir Ris

LOYANG

>HOLLAND RD & BUKIT TIMAH

Ever since the British housed their soldiers in the area, Holland Village has been a stronghold of affluent foreign residents. Today, the semicircle of bars and restaurants around Lorong Mambong and along Jl Merah Saga looks more like Sydney than Singapore.

Explore further afield and you'll find this area immediately west of the city is largely the domain of the prosperous. Dotted around the suburban streets, drawn to all the money, are small clusters of shops and restaurant-bar strips such as Greenwood Ave and Dempsey Rd, where former military barracks have been converted. In these areas you'll find the kind of neighbourhood vibe absent from much of the city centre.

Book-ending them are two of Singapore's most outstanding green spaces: the Botanic Gardens close to Orchard Rd and the Bukit Timah Nature Reserve rainforest to the west.

HOLLAND RD & BUKIT TIMAH

◉ SEE
National Orchid
Garden 1 G4
Singapore Botanic
Gardens 2 H5

◻ SHOP
da paolo
Gastronomie 3 D4
Galerie Cho Lón 4 D4
Holland Village
Shopping Centre 5 D4
Jones the Grocer 6 F5
Pantry Magic 7 D4
Red House Antiques 8 G5
Shang Antiques 9 F5

⊞ EAT
2am Dessert Bar 10 D4
Au Jardin Les
Amis 11 G4
Greenwood Fish
Market & Bistro 12 F1
Halia 13 G4
Holland Village
Market & Food
Centre 14 D4
Island Creamery 15 G2
Original Sin ....(see 3)
Picotin ....(see 26)
Samy's Curry
Restaurant 16 G5
Sebastien's 17 F1

▼ DRINK
Dempsey's Hut 18 G5
Hacienda 19 F5
L'Estaminet 20 F1
Red Dot Brewhouse 21 G5
The Old Brown Shoe 22 F2
The Wine Company 23 H3
The Wine Network 24 F5
Wala Wala 25 D4

★ PLAY
Horse City 26 D1
Shermay's Cooking
School ....(see 3)

Please see over for map

Former soldiers sharing memories at the Holland Village Market & Food Centre (p123)

SEE

BUKIT TIMAH NATURE RESERVE

☎ 6468 5736; www.nparks.gov
.sg; 177 Hindhede Dr; admission free;
🕑 8.30am-7pm; 🚌 170

Singapore's only surviving patch of primary rainforest has the dual honour of being its highest point – a dizzying 163m. Most walkers take the paved trail to the summit, but we suggest diving off along the North View, South View or Fern Valley paths for a distinctly out-of-Singapore experience.

MEMORIES AT OLD FORD FACTORY

☎ 6462 6724; 351 Upper Bukit Timah Rd; adult/child $3/2.50; 🕑 9am-5.30pm Mon-Sat, noon-5.30pm Sun; 🚌 170; ♿

Site of the humiliating British surrender to the Japanese in 1942, this museum, designed to appeal to young and old alike, tells the story of the Japanese occupation – a watershed period Singapore clearly doesn't want its youth to forget.

SINGAPORE BOTANIC GARDENS

☎ 6471 7361; www.sbg.org.sg; 1 Cluny Rd; Garden admission free, Orchid Garden adult/child $5/free; 🕑 5am-midnight; 🚌 7, 105, 123; ♿

Established in 1860, this wonderful 52-hectare park retains an aura of Victorian gentility, with its swan lake, symphony stage and themed gardens (including the National Orchid Garden). A late-afternoon stroll along its

NEIGHBOURHOODS

HOLLAND RD & BUKIT TIMAH

A

B

C

D

1

To Unique Seafood
Market (300m)

To Bukit Timah
Nature Reserve (1km);
Memories at Old Ford
Factory (1.5km)

26

2

Clementi

Ulu Pandan Rd

3

4

Dover

North Buona Vista Rd

Lorong Mambong

25

3

Jln Merah
Saga

4

10

7

Holland
Ave

Holland
Village

Commonwealth Ave

Dover Rd

Buona
Vista

5

Commonwealth

Ayer Rajah Expwy

6

See Southwest Singapore
Map pp130–1

E

To Bukit Timah
Saddle Club (500m);
Rider's Café (500m)

Greenwood Ave
12
20
F
Hillcrest Rd

Bukit Timah Rd

22

G

Adam Rd

H

Singapore Island
Country
Club

Pan-Island Expwy

1

Dunearn Rd

Rochor Canal

Jalan Serena
15

Cluny Park Rd

Dalvey Estate
23

3

Farrer Rd

Cluny Rd
Evans Rd

Nassim Rd

Galton Rd

Tyersall Rd

Holland Rd

Singapore
Botanic
Gardens

Tyersall Ave

Dalvey Gate Rd
11
1
13

4

See Orchard Rd
Map pp40–1

2

Nassim Hill

Holland Rd

Napier Rd

5

Dempsey Rd

21
8
16
9
Adley Rd

18

Minden Rd

Tanglin
Golf Course

24
19
6
Harding Rd

Tanglin Rd

Loewen Rd

Ridley Park

6

Queensway

Queenstown

The Singapore Botanic Gardens (p117) offers sanctuary at the edge of busy Orchard Rd

myriad paths, followed by a drink or dinner at Halia (p123) or Au Jardin Les Amis (p123) is one of the city's most memorable experiences.

SHOP

The Holland Rd area is a great alternative to the mall madness of the city, but you'll need to do a fair bit of legwork. Dempsey Rd was an enclave of Asian antiques, art and furniture long before the current restaurant boom, while Holland Village's old mall and small shops are a good hunting ground for the unusual.

🛍 DA PAOLO GASTRONOMIA
Food

☎ 6475 1323; 43 Jl Merah Saga;
🕘 9.30am-9pm; 🚌 7

Top-notch deli and the perfect place to fuel up for a shopping jaunt around Holland Village. Choose your gourmet pizza, salad, dessert, dip, bread or sandwich, then score one of the bench tables along the pavement for a picnic.

🛍 GALÉRIE CHO LÓN
Furniture, Collectables

☎ 6473 7922; 43 Jl Merah Saga;
🕘 11am-7.30pm Mon-Fri, 11am-8.30pm Sat, noon-7pm Sun; 🚌 7

Marrying the polish of a high-end lifestyle store with the chaotic jumble of an eccentric curio shop, Cho Lón always has the ability to surprise. Among the familiar range of Asian furniture, homewares and antiques you'll find a range of books, plus things such as old-style stitched leather footballs and antique kids' bicycles. A delight.

🅰 JONES THE GROCER *Food*
☎ 6476 1512; www.jonesthegrocer.com; Block 9, Dempsey Rd; ⏰ 9.30am-6pm Mon, 9am-11pm Tue-Sun; 🚌 7, 67, 174, then walk; ♿
Australian posh-nosh store and bistro dedicated to high-end edibles. Wildly popular with expats, it's worth visiting for its superbly smelly cheese room, though some of the produce is ex-

pensive (we noted high mark up on items readily available in local supermarkets).

🅰 PANTRY MAGIC *Cookware*
☎ 6471 0566; www.pantry-magic.com; 43 Jl Merah Saga; ⏰ 10am-9pm Sun-Thu, 10am-10pm Fri & Sat; 🚌 7; ♿
Neatly stacked with gleaming copper, stainless steel and cast iron (there are even miniature fondue sets), this is cookware so professional it makes you want to throw a tantrum.

🅰 RED HOUSE ANTIQUES *Antiques*
☎ 6474 6980; www.redhouseantiques.com.sg; 01-03, 26 Dempsey Rd; ⏰ 10.30am-6.30pm; 🚌 7, 67, 174; ♿
Specialist in Chinese antique furniture and restoration, Red House has been around for years and is

HOLLAND VILLAGE SHOPPING CENTRE

This ageing, slightly run-down **building** (Map pp118–19; 211 Holland Ave) is a magnet for expats and fashionable Singaporeans and a great place for an aimless browse among the arts, handicrafts, gifts, homewares and fashion outlets. Then top it off at one of the massage, reflexology or beauty salons on level 3 for a little pampering afterwards. Most stalls open around 10am and close between 8pm and 9.30pm.

Lim's Arts & Living (Shop 01, level 2) is a virtual encyclopedia of home furnishing, from kitsch model ships to classy Middle Eastern– and Asian-style lamps and chests. **Island & Archipelago** (Shop 05, level 2) has interesting retro, beachy-style dresses, while **EMF** (Shop 24, level 2) has a large selection of secondhand books for sale, rent or trade. **Framing Angie** (Shop 02, level 3) is a classy art gallery that'll also do a great job of framing pictures. For some beautiful and unusual wooden pots and vases, take a look at **Mango Wood Crafts** (Shop 08, level 3).

On the corner outside, check out newsstand, which has one of the largest range of newspapers and magazines in the city. This is Singapore, so it might not be long before it's decided Holland Village needs a shiny, spanking modern identikit mall to complement its new MRT station, and this little gem is torn down.

one of the most reliable dealers in the city. There are some magnificent old pieces on display, from the smallest chair to the most enormous doors and screens.

SHANG ANTIQUES *Antiques*
☎ 6388 8838; 01-04, 16 Dempsey Rd; 🕙 11am-6.30pm; 🚍 7, 67, 174; ♿
Specialising in antique religious artefacts from Cambodia, Laos, Thailand, India and Burma, as well as reproductions, there are items in here dating back nearly 2000 years, with price tags to match.

🍴 EAT
You'd hardly know it driving through the endless residential suburbs, but there is some

fantastic eating to be done in this area, concentrated around Holland Village, Dempsey Rd and Greenwood Ave. True to the style of these neighbourhoods, much of it is Western food, though if you explore a bit deeper there are plenty of cheap coffee shops and hawker centres around as well.

🍴 2AM DESSERT BAR
Bistro $$
☎ 6291 9727; www.2amdessertbar.com; 21a Lorong Liput, Holland Village; 4pm-2am Mon-Sat; 🚍 7; Ⓥ ♿
This unique eatery pairs beautifully crafted desserts with expertly chosen wines. Though a popular spot for late-night sweets and libation, its dinner menu (served all night) is amazing as well.

🍴 AU JARDIN LES AMIS
French $$$

☎ 6466 8812; EJH Corner House, Singapore Botanic Gardens, Cluny Rd; ⏱ noon-2pm Fri, 11.30am-2pm Sun, 7-9.30pm daily; 🚌 7, 105, 123, 174, 502; ♿

It's not difficult to see why it's at the top of many food lists. Combine a dreamy Botanic Gardens setting with traditional French fare (pâté de fois gras and truffles) with interlopers such as tiramisu and Iranian caviar. Bookings are essential.

🍴 GREENWOOD FISH MARKET & BISTRO *Seafood* $$

☎ 6467 4950; 34 Greenwood Ave; ⏱ noon-2.30pm & 6.30-10pm; 🚌 170; ♿

Outstandingly fresh, the potential meals here are either lying on a bed of ice, or crawling around in the tank inside. Well known for its fish and chips, it also has a $1 oyster night on Tuesdays. The fishmonger stays open from 10am to 10pm.

🍴 HALIA *International* $$$

☎ 6476 6711; www.halia.com.sg; Singapore Botanic Gardens, 1 Cluny Rd; ⏱ 11am-11pm Mon-Fri, 9am-11pm Sat & Sun; 🚌 7, 105, 123, 174, 502; ♿ Ⓥ ♿

With a location like this, nestled among the ginger plants in the botanic gardens, who needs good food? Fortunately, Halia provides that as well. Book a table on the verandah for a perfect romantic dinner, or come for its

English tea and cakes (3pm to 5pm Monday to Saturday).

🍴 HOLLAND VILLAGE MARKET & FOOD CENTRE
Hawker Centre $

Lor Mambong; ⏱ 10am-late; 🚌 7; ♿

Despite the signboard outside telling foreigners how to navigate hawker centres and describing different dishes, few venture from the pricier restaurants across the road. All the classics are here, from barbecue seafood to Katong laksa to fried *kway teow* (rice noodles).

🍴 ISLAND CREAMERY
Dessert $

☎ 6468 8859; 01-03 Serene Centre, 10 Jl Serene; ⏱ 11am-10pm; 🚌 174

Almost a religious shrine for many Singaporeans, who don't mind trekking out of their way to this tiny shop for its ice creams, sorbets and pies. Specialising in local flavours such as *teh tarik* (sweet Indian spiced tea), *cendol* (shaved

HUNGRY GO WHERE?
The website www.hungrygowhere.com offers independent reviews of the best (and worst) of Singapore's culinary scene. Want to know if that newly opened five-star restaurant is worth the money, or if that tiny hawker-centre stall is worth the queue? Chances are good that someone's written about it at HGW. If not, log in and add a review of your own!

iced and coconut milk dessert) and the wonderful Tiger beer sorbet, there are others devoted to its Horlicks and Nutella concoctions.

🍴 ORIGINAL SIN *Vegetarian* $$
☎ 6475 5605; 43 Jl Merah Saga;
🕑 lunch 11.30am-2.30pm Tue-Sun, dinner 6pm-10.15pm; 🚌 7; 🚻 Ⓥ 🚹
It must be pretty rare for a purely vegetarian restaurant to have so many ardent carnivorous admirers, but Original Sin's superb creations on an oft-changing menu, coupled with its long wine list and relaxed atmosphere devoid of precious-ness, have won many meat-eaters over – if only temporarily.

🍴 PICOTIN
European Bistro $$
☎ 6877 1191; www.picotin.com.sg; 100 Turf Club; 🕑 8-11am & noon-midnight;
🚌 171 from Orchard Rd; 🚻 🚹
This family-style place is part of the revamped Horse City and serves French cuisine. House specials include beef *bourguignon*,

poutine de porc and homemade black pudding. It also serves amazing full European breakfasts. Indoor and outdoor seating gives the restaurant – itself a renovated stable – atmosphere to spare.

🍴 RIDER'S CAFE *Bistro* $$
☎ 6466 9819; www.riderscafe.sg;
51 Fairways Dr; 🕑 8am-10pm Tue-Sun;
🚌 taxi; Ⓥ 🚹
This lovely restaurant is part of the exclusive Bukit Timah Saddle Club. Though the food is outstanding, portions are on the small side and service is a bit slow. Set in an old bungalow surrounded by meadows and horses, the atmosphere alone makes it worth the trip.

🍴 SAMY'S CURRY RESTAURANT *Indian* $$
☎ 6472 2080; Civil Service Club, Block 25, Dempsey Rd; 🕑 11am-11pm; 🚌 7, 77, 105, 106, 123, 174; Ⓥ 🚹
For 25 years, the ceiling fans spun above the banana leaves in this leafy, open-walled, timber-

---

WHAT'S IN A NAME?
Singapore loves acronyms, which pepper the speech of the average citizen and confuse visitors. (A cab driver might ask you something like: 'You wan go by which way: CTE or PIE? CTE very jam – ERP finish orredi. NDP practice finish and everyone go home watch EPL.') The city is also fond of prosaic titles. For example, a competition was held to name Changi Airport's new budget airline terminal. The winner: Budget Terminal. Meanwhile, the committee overseeing the development of Marina Bay hired branding and image specialists to come up with a name for the area. After much deliberation and great expense, they decided on...Marina Bay. And when media and pub-lishing giant SPH embarked on a mission to name its new paper...yes, it became the *New Paper*.

A BIT OF A BARRACKING

Dempsey Rd once felt like a real find, a hideaway of crumbling old military barracks occupied by antique shops, galleries, a couple of wine bars and the wonderful Samy's Curry Restaurant. Then Singapore's relentless developers got their mitts on it, 'rebranded' it Tanglin Village, and turned it into an 'exclusive' ghetto. The once deserted, peaceful streets are jammed with BMWs and Mercs, but don't let that fool you. In our experience, the service at much-hyped restaurants Oosh and **Red Dot Brewhouse** (p126) was rotten – though the bar at the latter is worth a visit for its craft beers. However, the area still hides gems such as **Hacienda** (p126) and Dempsey Rd stalwarts **The Wine Network** (p127) and **Samy's Curry** (left).

shuttered colonial throwback. Then, as the area developed around them, some genius decided it was time for the timber shutters to go. The food is still magnificent, but much of the atmosphere has gone.

SEBASTIEN'S French $$$

☎ 6465 1980; 12 Greenwood Ave;
🕑 6.30-10pm Tue-Sun, 9-11am & noon-2.30pm Sat & Sun; 🚍 66, 67, 174; ♿ 🚼
Cosy, relaxed French bistro with a genial eponymous owner, serving up commendable classics such as *boeuf bourguignon* (pot-roast beef in red wine) and *escargot* (snails) baked in mushrooms, plus an outstanding collection of cheeses.

UNIQUE SEAFOOD MARKET
Seafood $$

☎ Ah Yat 6883 2112, Owen 6875 1895;
Grandstand, 200 Turf Club Rd; 🕑 Ah Yat 11.30am-2.30pm & 5.30-10.30pm, Owen 11.30am-10.30pm; 🚍 66, 67, 174, then walk, free Turf City shuttle from Toa Payoh Bus Interchange; 🚼

When they called this unique, they weren't lying. Set in the grandstand of the old racecourse, it features a seafood market where you choose your victims from more than 50 tanks, before retiring to either the Hong Kong–style Ah Yat or pan-Asian Owen seafood restaurants. A memorable experience, particularly at weekends.

🍸 DRINK

DEMPSEY'S HUT Pub

☎ 6473 9609; 130E Minden Rd;
🕑 noon-1am Sun-Thu, noon-2am Fri & Sat; 🚍 7, 123, 174; ♿ 🚼
Nestled among the trees, away from the Beamers and Mercs jostling to park at Dempsey Rd, long-time resident Dempsey's Hut is refreshingly unpretentious: a no-frills outdoor pub, crumbling at the edges, with a pool table, relaxed atmosphere, relatively cheap beers and some surprisingly good food (try the New Zealand lamb).

▼ HACIENDA *Bar, Restaurant*
☎ 6476 2922; 13A Dempsey Rd;
🕐 5pm-2am Mon-Sat, 1pm-2am Sun;
🚌 7, 67, 123, 174; ♿

One of the best bars around the Dempsey Rd area to kick off the shoes in the garden after a long hot day, sink a few mojitos or draught beers under the trees and contemplate the evening sky – at least until the band comes on.

▼ L'ESTAMINET *Bar, Restaurant*
☎ 6465 1911; 4 Greenwood Ave;
🕐 noon-10.30pm; 🚌 66, 67, 174

Like Oosters (p62), L'Estaminet is heavily stocked with a wide selection of Belgian beers, but the bar has a more rustic feel, more likely to be populated by shorts and T-shirts than shirts and trousers. It also serves up some superb wood-fired pizzas. Head to Sebastien's (p125) for dessert afterwards.

▼ RED DOT BREWHOUSE *Microbrewery*
☎ 6475 0500; 25A Dempsey Rd;
🕐 noon-11pm Sun-Thu, noon-1am Fri & Sat; 🚌 7, 67, 123, 174

This microbrewery is the product of one Singaporean's passion for beer, and a fine pursuit we say, as his beers are all pretty damn good. Red Dot also serves an excellent assortment of rather high-class bistro cuisine – try its all-vegetarian shiitake mushroom burger. The setting, in a quiet part of Dempsey, can't be beat.

WORTH THE TRIP

Not as manic as the track in Hong Kong, but nevertheless the **Singapore Turf Club** (☎ 6879 1000; www.turfclub.com.sg; 1 Turf Club Ave; air-con/nonair-con $7/3, private lounge $20; Ⓜ Kranji; ♿) is a great day out and a rare chance to see Singaporeans getting worked up.

There is a choice of seating in the four-storey grandstand: an open nonair-con area, an air-con area and the @Hibiscus lounge – though there's a strict dress code in there and anyone wearing jeans, open shoes or missing a collar at the neck will not be allowed in. Women get off lighter, but still require closed shoes.

For the best atmosphere, head for the sweaty cheap seats to cheer on your nag among the serious punters and dodgy characters.

All betting is, you guessed it, government controlled and the minimum bet is $5. Odds are deceptive: 5-1 odds, for example, means you win $5 for every $5 unit you bet, not $5 for every dollar, as in other places.

Races take place on Wednesday and Friday evenings, starting at 6.30pm, and on Saturdays and Sundays, starting at 1.45pm. Check the website for the calendar.

Massive sums of money pass through the windows on race days, which makes you wonder why there was such a fuss about the casinos. The Turf Club is right next to Kranji MRT station.

▼ THE OLD BROWN SHOE *Pub*
☎ 6468 4626; 619F Bukit Timah Rd;
🕑 4pm-midnight Mon-Fri, 4pm-1am Sat & Sun; 🚌 66, 67, 174; ♿
Classic British-style pub that gets especially jammed on Wednesday nights for its pub quiz, which draws competitive types from far outside the pub's usual Bukit Timah catchment area.

▼ THE WINE COMPANY
Wine Bar
☎ 6732 6698; Evans Lodge, 26 Evans Rd;
🕑 noon-midnight Mon-Thu, noon-1am Fri & Sat, 11am-11pm Sun; 🚌 66, 67, 174
Casual, relaxed, unstuffy wine bar in a quiet location opposite the National University of Singapore sports grounds. Places particular emphasis on offering 'affordable' wines, principally from South Africa.

▼ THE WINE NETWORK
Wine Bar
☎ 6479 2280; Block 13, Dempsey Rd;
🕑 11am-midnight Sun-Thu, 11am-1am Fri & Sat; 🚌 7, 123, 174; ♿
An old favourite of Dempsey Rd aficionados whose patronage predates the area's recent yuppi-fication. Sit and pine for the good old days over a large wine list in the bare-brick, barrel-scented in-terior, or on the peaceful wooden deck outside. Order some cheese

platters to ward off your hunger before dinner at Samy's Curry Restaurant (p124).

▼ WALA WALA *Cafe, Bar*
☎ 6462 4288; 31 Lor Mambong;
🕑 4pm-1am Mon-Thu, 3pm-2am Fri & Sat, 3pm-1am Sun; 🚌 7
Large, raucous but friendly, Wala Wala has been a long-standing favourite with the young expat crowd for its breezy vibe and its live-music bar upstairs, where the focus is on danceable, singable, air-punchable tunes.

⭐ PLAY

◻ HORSE CITY
Sports & Leisure Facility
☎ 6463 6012; www.horsecity.com.sg;
100 Turf Club Rd; pony rides $10, riding lessons $20, 1hr trail rides $80; 🕑 8am-7pm; 🚌 171 from Orchard Rd; ♿
A family oriented sports and leisure area with equestrian leanings, Horse City's major draw is its public riding facility, offering pony rides for children and trail rides for adults, as well as carriage rides and riding lessons. Other facilities include a gym, a petting zoo, a spa, a yoga studio, a children's gymnastics gym, a dance hall and even studios teaching *muay thai* kickboxing. Horse City is also the home of Picotin restaurant (p124).

>SOUTHWEST SINGAPORE

Bisected by the roaring, truck-laden Ayer Rajah Expressway and home to Singapore's mighty container terminals and industrial parks, this corner of the city is often overlooked by visitors, who pass through only to take the cable car between Mt Faber and Sentosa.

But there is another side to the area. Hidden among all the economic activity are two of the country's best urban retreats – Kent Ridge Park and Labrador Nature Reserve – which, despite their absorbing historical sites and fantastic views, are virtually deserted during the week.

The Sentosa gateway area has had a massive injection of life with the opening of the vast waterfront Vivocity shopping and entertainment mall and, across the road, the brilliantly converted St James Power Station, which houses one of the city's most popular bar complexes.

SOUTHWEST SINGAPORE

🅒 SEE
Kent Ridge Park 1 C3
Labrador Secret
   Tunnels 2 E6
NUS Museums 3 B2
Reflections at Bukit
   Chandu 4 D4

🅗 SHOP
Vivocity 5 H6

🍴 EAT
Faber Hill Bistro 6 G5
Imperial Herbal
   Restaurant ....(see 5)
Jewel Box 7 G5
Peramakan 8 F5
Villa Bali 9 E4

🍸 DRINK
Altivo & Glass Bar ....(see 6)
Colbar 10 D2

Jewel Box ....(see 7)
Privé 11 F6
St James Power
   Station 12 H6

⭐ PLAY
Haw Par Villa 13 B3
Mt Faber Park 14 G5

Please see over for map

◉ SEE
◉ KENT RIDGE PARK
Vigilante Dr; ⏱ 24hr; 🚌 200, then walk

Commanding sweeping views over the port, outer islands and Indonesia beyond, it's astonishing that Kent Ridge Park is so deserted. But that's also what makes it one of the best urban escapes in Singapore, because you have kilometres of paths and the treetop boardwalk pretty much to yourself. Check out Reflections at Bukit Chandu (p132) while you're there.

◉ LABRADOR NATURE RESERVE
Labrador Villa Rd; ⏱ 24hr; Ⓜ HarbourFront, then bus 408 (Sat & Sun), taxi

Combining historical sites, long trails through a forest area rich in bird life, great views from Singapore's only sea cliffs and a beachfront park, Labrador Park is well worth spending an afternoon at. Examine the old British guns, hike through the jungle, visit the Secret Tunnels (below) and the pillbox on the beach, then have a picnic nearby.

◉ LABRADOR SECRET TUNNELS
☎ 8282 4500; Labrador Villa Rd, Labrador Nature Reserve; adult/child $8/5; ⏱ 1-6pm; Ⓜ HarbourFront, then bus 408 (Sat & Sun), taxi

GETTING THERE & AROUND
> **Bus** – 408 from HarbourFront MRT runs along the main artery through the area.

A series of storage and armament bunkers built by the British in the 1880s, the Secret Tunnels, incredibly, remained undiscovered for 50 years after WWII, until they were unearthed when work began on turning Labrador into a nature reserve. Small, but fascinating, there are displays of artefacts left behind when the British abandoned the tunnels in 1942, as well as the buckled and caved-in walls from a direct hit from a Japanese bomb.

◉ NUS MUSEUM
☎ 6516 8817; www.nus.edu.sg/museum; University Cultural Centre, 50 Kent Ridge Cres, National University of Singapore; admission free; ⏱ 10am-7.30pm Tue-Sat, 10am-6pm Sunday; Ⓜ Clementi, then bus 96 or taxi; ♿ 🍴

Located on the campus of the National University of Singapore (NUS), these three small but exquisite galleries hold some fine collections. One gallery focuses on Chinese art, another on art from South & Southeast Asia, and another features the works of Singaporean artist Ng Eng Teng.

Queenstown
See Holland Rd
& Bukit Timah
Map pp118–19

See Orchard Rd
Map pp40–1

E

F

G

H

1

Ridley Park

Grange Rd

Chatsworth Rd

Margaret Rd

Queenstown
M

Tanglin Rd

Singapore River

2

Tiong Bahru Rd

Alexandra Rd

Queensway

Redhill
M

Delta
Stadium

Tiong
Bahru
Park

3

Alexandra
Hospital

Jl Bukit Merah

Henderson Rd

Henderson
Park

Lower Delta Rd

Tiong
Bahru
M

Alexandra Rd

Jl Bukit Merah

4

9

Mt Faber
Park

Lower Delta Rd

5

14

6

7

Mt Faber
(116m)

8

To Ya Hua Rou
Ga Cha (700m)

Labrador
Nature
Reserve

Port Rd

Telok Blangah Rd

World
Trade
Centre

HarbourFront
M

Pulau
Keppel

11

5

12

Gateway Ave

6

Keppel Harbour

Jardine
Steps

⚑ REFLECTIONS AT BUKIT CHANDU

☎ 6375 2510; www.s1942.org.sg; 31K Pepys Rd; adult/child $2/1; ⏰ 9am-5pm Tue-Sun; 🚌 10, 30, 143; ♿

Commemorating the last stand of the Malay Regiment against the Japanese in 1942, and an ode to the old kampong days that have vanished from Singapore. Combines first-hand accounts, artefacts such as old guns and helmets, films and dramatisations to describe the tragic and brutal battle that almost wiped the regiment out.

🍴 EAT

🍴 FABER HILL BISTRO
Western $$

☎ 6377 9688; 101 Mt Faber Rd; ⏰ 9am-1am Sun-Tue, 9am-2am Wed-Sat; Ⓜ HarbourFront, then cable car, bus 409 (Sat & Sun), or walk; ♿ 🚼

The high canopy makes it feel a little like you're inside a wedding marquee, but with views like this from Mt Faber Hill you'll only be looking outwards. The steaks and pastas are just good enough to complement the twinkling skyline.

🍴 IMPERIAL HERBAL RESTAURANT *Chinese* $$

☎ 6337 0491; 03-08, Lobby G, Vivocity; ⏰ 11.30am-2.30pm & 6-10.15pm Mon-Fri, 11.30am-5pm & 6pm-10.15pm Sat & Sun; Ⓜ HarbourFront; ♿ Ⓥ

Feeling a little under? Have your pulse checked, tongue examined and physical ailments remedied and your body rebalanced with a precise prescription of herbal soups, double-boiled chickens and other more esoteric ingredients.

🍴 PERAMAKAN *Peranakan* $$

☎ 6375 5563; L3 Keppel Club, 10 Bukit Chermin Rd; ⏰ 11.30am-3pm & 6-10pm; Ⓜ HarbourFront, then bus 93

Run by a genial couple of cooking enthusiasts, this paragon of

---

WORTH THE TRIP

Staggeringly large, the waterfront **Vivocity** (☎ 6377 6860; 1 HarbourFront Walk; ⏰ 10am-10pm; Ⓜ HarbourFront; ♿) megamall is Singapore's largest, and offers a viable alternative to pavement-pounding on Orchard Rd, though its broad, squat design (by Japanese architect Toyo Ito) means there's still a prodigious amount of walking to do. There are dozens of ubiquitous fashion chains such as Diesel, Hang Ten and Esprit (and locals such as M)phosis) as well as smaller boutiques. Electronics giants such as Denki and Challenger also have a heavy presence. The excellent Page One bookshop is a rival to Kinokuniya in Orchard Rd, while the Golden Village cineplex is also Singapore's largest, with luxury Gold Class, GVMax and Cinema Europa cinemas. At night the waterfront side resembles a lower key version of Sydney's Darling Harbour, with top-end restaurants and a few lounge bars catching the evening breeze.

homestyle Baba-Nonya cuisine has migrated from its spiritual Joo Chiat home, but the classics such as *sambal* (spicy shrimp paste) squid and *rendang* (spicy coconut curry) remain as good as ever.

🍴 THE JEWEL BOX

Wine & Dine $$$

☎ 6377 9688; 109 Mt Faber Rd; www .mountfaber.com.sg; Ⓜ HarbourFront, then free shuttle

A collection of four wining and dining options housed in one architecturally stunning building atop Mt Faber, all offering gourmet cuisine and cocktails with a panoramic view for the smart-dress set. The phone number above will connect you to your eatery of choice to make reservations.

🍴 YA HUA ROU GU CHA

Chinese $

☎ 6222 9610; 7 Keppel Rd, PSA Tanjong Pagar Complex; ⏰ 7am-midnight; Ⓜ Tanjong Pagar

There's no such thing as 'location, location, location' when it comes to hawker food. Singaporeans would crawl through a sewage pipe if there were a good meal at the end of it, so the positioning of this famous *bak kut teh* (pork-rib soup) joint next to the port and beside an expressway doesn't stop the multitudes from coming to sip peppery broth and gnaw on bones.

KAMPONG DAYS

Fifty years ago the view from Mt Faber, Kent Ridge and Labrador Parks would have been vastly different. Until the 1950s, most Singaporeans lived in single storey homes in their kampong (traditional Malay village) on these hills – and countless other places – but population pressures and land scarcity saw them forced out. Singaporeans remain sentimental about the kampong but, as an old Malay veteran says in the documentary at **Reflections at Bukit Chandu** (opposite), 90% of them now live in 'comfortable HDB flats'. (Of course, he wasn't told to say they are 'comfortable'!)

🍸 DRINK

ALTIVO & GLASS BAR *Bar*

☎ 6377 9688; 109 Mt Faber Rd; ⏰ 9am-1am Sun-Tue, 9am-3am Wed-Sat; Ⓜ HarbourFront, then cable car, bus 409 (Sat & Sun), or walk; ♿

Part of the small complex atop Mt Faber Hill that sucks in the cable car and spits it out towards Sentosa, the Altivo outdoor lounge and impossibly hip indoor Glass Bar are both magical spots to watch dusk slide into night over the sea below.

🍸 COLBAR *Bar, Cafe*

☎ 6779 4859; 9A Whitchurch Rd; ⏰ 11am-11.30pm Tue-Sun; 🚌 100, 123, 147, then walk; ♿

Something of an institution, Colbar attracts a loyal crowd of weekend regulars drawn to the bare-bones decor, friendly service, wanton Sunday drunkenness and hangover-friendly fry-ups and curries.

🍸 PRIVÉ
Bar, Restaurant
☎ 6776 0777; www.prive.com.sg; Keppel Bay Dr; ⏱ noon-3pm & 6.30-11.30pm Mon-Fri, 6.30-11.30pm Sat; Ⓜ HarbourFront, then taxi

Located on an island out in the middle of Keppel Harbour, with the city on one side and Sentosa on the other, you couldn't ask for a better location for evening drinks. Attracts an affluent, well-dressed crowd, with guest DJs and occasional live music. The attached restaurant serves French-American cuisine and specialises in steaks, seafood and pasta dishes.

ST JAMES POWER STATION

Converting a 1920s coal-fired power station into an entertainment complex took huge amounts of money and a fair scoopful of design talent. All the bars and clubs are interconnected, so one cover charge (men/women $12/10 on weekdays, $20/15 on weekends) gets you access to all of them. On Wednesday ladies' nights, men pay $20 but women get in free. Several bars – the Bellini Room, Gallery Bar, Lobby Bar and Peppermint Park – have no cover charge at all. The minimum age is 18 for women and 23 for men at all except Powerhouse, where the age is 18 for both.

> **Bellini Room** (⏱ 8pm-3am Mon-Thu, 8pm-4am Fri & Sat) Cool, stylish jazz and swing bar lit in deep red and blue, with a live band doing sets throughout the night. Great fun.

> **Dragonfly** (⏱ 6pm-6am) Hugely popular Cantopop and Mandopop club, with live bands (featuring regulation sexily clad girls and spiky-haired boys) and a curious PVC pipe ceiling design. Expect to be the only foreigner in here.

> **Gallery Bar** (⏱ 8pm-3am Mon-Thu, 8pm-4am Fri & Sat) Ingeniously designed glass-walled bar offering views into the four main clubs but shielded from the noise of each. Great spot to retreat, relax and decide where to go next.

> **Mono** (⏱ 6pm-6am) Karaoke bar with 10 private rooms, done out like a horror-movie French bordello.

> **Movida** (⏱ 6pm-3am) Decked out like a '70s disco, this Latin dance club features an excellent, eye-catching, thoroughly danceable band from Paraguay. The best of the lot.

> **Peppermint Park** (⏱ 6pm-3am Mon-Thu, 6pm-4am Fri & Sat) Outdoor chill-out area with a bar, large day beds and swing seats.

> **Powerhouse** (⏱ 8pm-4am Wed, Fri & Sat) Industrial design and a huge dance space aimed at a younger crowd.

> **The Boiler Room** (⏱ 8.45pm-3am Mon-Sat) Straight-up, no frills rock and pop club, with a Filipino band performing Western hits to a largely table-bound audience.

The Bellini Room is one of eight themed rooms at the ultrahip St James Power Station

 VILLA BALI *Bar, Restaurant*
☎ 9750 2140; www.littlebali.com;
9A Lock Rd, Gillman Village; 🕑 4pm-
midnight Mon-Thu, 4pm-2am Fri & Sat;
🚌 57, 195; 🚹
The highlight of this relaxed
garden bar is the private wooden
platforms, where you can recline
back on some cushions, sink a few
drinks and sample some decent
Indian snacks.

⭐ PLAY

⭐ **HAW PAR VILLA** *Theme Park*
☎ 9451 7685; www.singaporesights.
com/sight/haw-par-villa; 262 Pasir Panjang Rd; 🕑 9am-7pm; Ⓜ HarbourFront,
then bus 10, 30 or 188; 🚹 🚹
This weird and wonderful
psychedelic sculpture park offers
visitors the chance to experience

first hand Chinese history and
mythology, and even a taste of the
afterlife.

⭐ **MT FABER PARK** *Park*
☎ 6377 9688; www.mountfaber.com;
109 Mt Faber Rd; Ⓜ HarbourFront, then
cable car, bus 409 (Sat & Sun), or walk
Standing 166m above the south
fringe of the city, the Pulau
Brani port and HarbourFront, Mt
Faber's steeply terraced trails wind
through humming forest, past
strategically positioned view-
points. Run by a leisure group, it's
a lot busier and more commercial
than Kent Ridge or Labrador
parks, but it also boasts bars with
some of best views in the city. The
exhilarating **cable car** (adult/child return
$11.90/6.50; 🕑 8.30pm-11pm) is the best
way to get to and from the hill.

>JURONG

It's hard to decide whether placing a whole gamut of child-friendly attractions in a working-class industrial suburb was inspired or bizarre, but nonetheless there they are. The world-class Jurong Bird Park, Science Centre, indoor snow slope and Imax cinema can keep the little ones (and yourself) occupied for a couple of days, but it's a fair hike out from the city centre and, once you're there, there isn't a good deal else in the way of shops or restaurants.

However, one saving grace is the superb Hilltop Japanese Restaurant, a short walk up from the Jurong Bird Park, plus a half-decent Peranakan joint in the Science Centre.

JURONG

● SEE
Chinese Garden **1** D1
Japanese Garden **2** E2
Jurong Bird Park **3** A4
Jurong Lookout Tower ...**4** B4
Science Centre
    Singapore **5** F2

🍴 EAT
Hilltop Japanese
    Restaurant **6** B4

⭐ PLAY
Omni-Theatre **7** E2
Snow City **8** E2

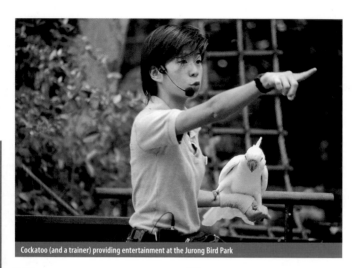

Cockatoo (and a trainer) providing entertainment at the Jurong Bird Park

◉ SEE

◉ CHINESE & JAPANESE GARDENS

☎ 6261 3632; 1 Chinese Garden Rd;
🕙 6am-11pm; Ⓜ Chinese Garden; ♿
A thoroughly pleasant re-creation of a classical Chinese garden, set against a backdrop of public housing, this is probably best combined with a trip to the Jurong Bird Park and/or Science Centre. The highlight is the truly outstanding bonsai collection (the centrepiece tree is 300 years old!). The neighbouring Japanese Garden is rather sparse and hardly worth the walk.

◉ JURONG BIRD PARK

☎ 6265 0022; www.birdpark.com.sg; 2 Jurong Hill; adult/child $18/12, panorail $5/3; 🕙 8.30am-5.30pm Ⓜ Boon Lay, then bus 194 or 251
Boasting one of the largest bird collections in the world, the Jurong Bird Park features a number of enthralling open-concept aviaries. Don't miss the Waterfall Aviary (with the largest artificial falls on earth), the African Wetlands and the Lori Loft, as well as the Birds of Prey show. Check the website for specials combining admission to the Bird Park, Singapore Zoo and Night Safari (p48).

Jack & Rai
Musical Duo

Best neighbourhood for club-hopping? Clarke Quay definitely, because it houses so many excellent live-music venues. We also like the *mojitos* at Cuba Libre (p76). **Best bar or club for an intimate night out?** The whole Holland Village area is great for an intimate night out. The area has a lot of restaurants, and if you want to go for a drink afterwards there are a lot of places to go. We really like to bring our dates to 2am Dessert Bar (p122) then go to Wala Wala (p127) to chill out. **Best venue for dancing?** We don't dance that much, but the Butter Factory (p81) is a good place for dancing. **Any open mic nights?** A place called Actor's Bar (p75) in Boat Quay has sort of an open mic karaoke night. The band will play requests and you can get up and sing. **Traditional Singaporean hangover cure?** Jack: Two Panadol and a can of 100 Plus! Rai: I've heard a Guinness stout with a raw egg in it works, but I've yet to try it.

NEIGHBOURHOODS

JURONG

People experimenting with interactive displays at Science Centre Singapore

◎ JURONG LOOKOUT TOWER

Jurong Hill; Ⓜ Jurong East, then bus 194, 251

A curious relic of the 1970s (as if you couldn't tell), this viewing tower boasts a stained-glass ceiling and a futuristic night-time view over the lights and flaming stacks of the Jurong Island industrial zone. Take a hike up after the Jurong Bird Park (p138) and eat at Hilltop Japanese Restaurant (opposite) in the basement afterwards.

◎ SCIENCE CENTRE SINGAPORE

☎ 6425 2500; www.science.edu.sg; 15 Science Centre Rd; adult/child $6/3, with IMAX movie $12.80/6.40; ⏰ 10am-6pm Tue-Sun, Mon during school holidays; Ⓜ Jurong East; ♿

A huge collection of interactive exhibits covering outer space, earth sciences, the human body and visual illusions, as well as frequent travelling exhibitions, makes this one of the most visited places in Singapore. The outdoor interactive sculpture/water park alone is worth the trip – bring bathing suits and towels for the little ones.

V

NEIGHBOURHOODS

JURONG

🍴 EAT

🍴 HILLTOP JAPANESE RESTAURANT *Japanese* $$

☎ 6266 3522; 2 Jurong Hill;
🕑 11.30am-9.45pm; Ⓜ Jurong East,
then bus 194, 251; ♿

As if finding a Japanese restaurant here isn't strange enough, it turns out to be a Japanese-Indonesian restaurant to boot. Most diners come for the excellent teppanyaki, a few Asahis and a climb up the observation tower afterwards, though you can get your *nasi goreng* (fried rice) and *gado gado* (vegetable salad with peanut sauce) too.

⭐ PLAY

⭐ OMNI-THEATRE *Cinema*

☎ 6425 2500; www.omnitheatre.com
.sg; 21 Jurong Town Hall Rd; adult/
child $10/5; 🕑 10am-8pm Tue-Sun;
Ⓜ Jurong East

This vast domed cinema is an unforgettable experience, showing short 15- to 20-minute movies on anything from African wildlife to space exploration and simulated thrill rides, on a huge

---

WORTH THE TRIP

The **Sungei Buloh Wetland Reserve** (☎ 6794 1401; www.sbwr.org.sg; 301 Neo Tiew Crescent; Mon-Fri admission free, adult/child Sat, Sun, public & school holidays $1/0.50; 🕑 7.30am-7pm Mon-Sat, 7am-7pm Sun; Ⓜ Kranji, then bus 925) is an 87-hectare nature reserve in far northwest Singapore overlooking the Strait of Johor, and home to 140 species of birds. It's been declared a nature reserve and recognised as a sanctuary of international importance as part of the East Asia Flyway.

The best time for viewing birds is before 10am, and if you go on a weekday the reserve is blissfully serene. Be prepared for encounters with several monitor lizards, some of them unnervingly large, and sightings of playful otter families hunting fish. There are also, apparently, saltwater crocodiles in the area, though sightings (thankfully) seem to be rare.

From the visitors centre trails lead around ponds and mangroves to small hides decked out with signboards that'll help you identify the different species. There's also a three-storey aerie. Allow three hours to do the reserve justice.

Free guided tours begin at 9.30am and 3.30pm on Saturdays. On other days, tours have to be prebooked and cost $50 per group. Audiovisual shows on the park's flora and fauna are held at 9am, 11am, 1pm, 3pm and 5pm (hourly between 9am and 5pm on Sunday).

On weekdays, the bus stops at the end of Neo Tiew Cres, a 10-minute walk from the park. On Sundays, the bus goes right to the park entrance.

V

NEIGHBOURHOODS

JURONG

BEERS BY THE BOWSPRIT

As far away as it's possible to get from the city, **Raffles Marina** (☎ 6861 8000; www.rafflesmarina.com.sg; 10 Tuas West Dr; M Boon Lay, then bus 192, 193) is a surreal world of clanging halyards, cawing birds and salty stories out in the industrial wastelands of Singapore's far west. Temporary home to travelling yachties and a few boat-dwelling residents, it's a great place to sit at sunset over dinner with a few beers — even better if you have a few seaman's tales to share. Have a dockside dinner at **Marina Bistro** (☎ 6869 2299; ☙ 8am-10pm), then a beer at the **Discovery Pub** (☎ 6869 2277; ☙ noon-midnight). There's also a bowling alley and a billiard room.

screen that envelopes you on your reclining seat.

⭐ **SNOW CITY** *Playground*
☎ 6560 2306; www.snowcity.com.sg; adult/child $16/14; ☙ 9.45am-5.15pm Tue-Sun; M Jurong East
Recent arrivals from winter climates might fail to see the appeal here, but throwing yourself down a snow-covered 70m slope on a huge inner tube in -5°C temperatures until you lose all feeling in your extremities is a big draw if you live most of your life in 90% humidity. Kids will definitely love it while adults can sneak off to the bar. Sessions last an hour and tickets get you entry into the Science Centre Singapore (p140) next door.

The view of Fullerton Hotel across the Singapore River

WALKING TOURS

COLONIAL NIGHT WALK

There are three very good reasons to explore the Colonial District at night: you don't get baked in the sun, the traffic is significantly lighter and the buildings are beautifully lit.

Start around 7pm, taking exit B from **Dhoby Ghaut MRT (1)**. Walk left along Penang Rd and where the road bends to the left, nip across and climb the stairs next to the Fort Canning Tunnel exit. Down Fort Canning Rd on the

distance 3.5km **duration** 50 minutes ▶ **start** Ⓜ Dhoby Ghaut ● **end** Boat Quay right, the **Wesley Methodist Church (2)** dates back to 1908 (the original stained-glass windows were recovered from the wreckage of the Japanese retreat).

Next up is the magnificent **National Museum of Singapore (3**; p70) – add 10 minutes for a wander through the building, saving a visit for later.

A stroll between the **Singapore Management University (4)** buildings provides a modern counterpoint to the area's Victorian structures. Turn right – noting the **Church of the Good Shepherd (5)** to the left – cross Stamford Rd into dimly lit Armenian St, past the **Substation (6**; p79) theatre (time for a drink around the back?) and the **Peranakan Museum (7**; p70).

Head left into Coleman St and past the stately **Philatelic Museum (8)**, **Masonic Hall (9)** and, hidden among the trees to the left, the **Armenian Church (10)**.

Cross Hill St, continue down Coleman St, then turn right into North Bridge Rd. After the marble **Parliament (11)** emerges to the left, you're reward-ed with a wonderful view of the river, the rumbling bumboats and lights of **Boat Quay (12)**, dwarfed by the thicket of skyscrapers in the financial district.

Look back at the **Supreme Court (13)**, then descend the steps to the promenade. Pass the **statue of Sir Stamford Raffles (14)**, marking the spot he first landed in Singapore, **Indochine (15)** and the **Asian Civilisations Museum (16**; p67), before crossing **Cavenagh Bridge (17)** – check out the cats to the right of the bridge. Turn left along the river, past the **Fullerton Hotel (18)** diners, cross the **Anderson Bridge (19)**, then dive down to the left of the **Waterboat House (20)** and walk under the Esplanade Drive bridge to the **Merlion Park (21)** for a great view of the Esplanade theatres, Suntec City, Singapore Flyer and the gargantuan Marina Bay Sands, which should be finished by the time you read this.

After a break, double back, retrace your steps to Boat Quay and reward yourself with a drink at the Archipelago microbrewery (p76) on Circular Rd.

Take a break from the manic city at idyllic Fort Canning Park (p39)

SINGAPORE NATURE TRAIL

Begin at **MacRitchie Reservoir Park (1)** – carrying lots of water – then follow the path around the right side of the reservoir until you reach a fork. Take the boardwalk to the left, keeping an eye out for macaques (keep any food hidden, or they can get aggressive), monitor lizards, flying lemurs and terrapins.

Follow the water's edge until the boardwalk ends and connects you to the **MacRitchie Nature Trail (2)** track. After 2km you hit a paved road at the **Island Country Club (3)**.

Turn left along the road, then take the next road left, which ends at the Kallang Service Reservoir. Follow the signs to the **Treetop Walk (4)**, cross the bridge, looking out for sunbathing snakes, then follow the boardwalk through the forest.

Spot primates at the MacRitchie Reservoir Park

distance 12km **duration** Four hours ▶ **start** MacRitchie Reservoir Park ⏺ **end** MacRitchie Reservoir Park

Turn right onto the Sime Track until you reach the **Jelutong Tower (5)** – climb for a view.

Follow the track until you reach a sign for the Jering Trail, which hugs the edge of the reservoir. Look out for a mysterious **Chinese tombstone (6)** – no one knows who is buried there.

Finally, cross the strange **zigzag bridge (7)** and climb the small hill for a rewarding drink at the food centre back where you started.

WALKING TOURS

CHINATOWN

Emerge from **Chinatown MRT (1)** on Pagoda St and battle through the stalls to Trengganu St, where you turn right. After crossing Temple St, look up at the rickety balustrade running around the early-20th-century building to your left. Grab a sausage from **Erich's Wuerstelstand (2**; p57) and turn left down Sago St until you reach South Bridge Rd. Turn right, admiring the **Buddha Tooth Relic Temple(3**; p51), then cross the street and head to the **Maxwell Rd Hawker Centre (4**; p59). Turn left up Kadayanallur St, passing the gothic **Scarlet Hotel (5)**, then follow the road past the old clan headquarters and renovated shophouses to Ann Siang Hill. Walk up the hill, down the iron spiral staircase to your left, then turn right, descending to Amoy St, peeking in at the **Siang Cho Keong Temple (6)**. Turn left into Telok Ayer St, passing the **Al-Abrar Mosque (7)** before reaching the beautiful **Thian Hock Keng Temple (8**; p54). Continue on past **Telok Ayer Garden (9)** and the restored **Nagore Durgha Shrine (10)**, traverse Cross St, then duck through the ancient doorway of the **Fuk Tak Ch'i Museum (11)** emerging, surreally, out the back door into the air-conditioned comfort of Far East Sq.

distance 2km **duration** 40 minutes ▶ **start** Ⓜ Chinatown ● **end** Far East Sq

>THE NEW SINGAPORE

Ultramodern and efficient Dhoby Ghaut MRT Station

THE NEW SINGAPORE

Change is hardly new to Singapore – the island has been in a near constant state of flux since it was founded, but today's city is undergoing the kind of social and physical transition it hasn't seen since the manic construction boom of the '60s and '70s. The closed, tightly controlled society for which it became famous is looking increasingly fragile. Though the government's ruthless grip on political power is unlikely to be loosened, Singapore simply cannot survive by looking inwards, so it is being forced to try and shed the insular parochialism of old and remake itself in the image of the cosmopolitan, freewheeling metropolises around the world it aspires to emulate.

The principal reasons are, of course, economic. Manufacturing – once the country's engine room – is migrating to cheaper climes, so Singapore is having to reinvent itself fast as a hub for everything from financial services to aviation to biomedical engineering to tourism, conventions, entertainment and sports. And to support this globalised economic base, it needs to import people – another two million of them, in the government's estimation.

It's a change that promises to utterly transform the city and, possibly, the ever-widening income gap will mean many people, most of them Singaporeans, are left behind. It will be intriguing to see what effect this has on the city's rock-hard social stability.

Dempsey Rd (p125) is home to flashy cars and posh restaurants

INTEGRATED RESORTS

Singapore is accustomed to large-scale construction projects, but few have generated the kind of interest now focused on its two casinos (known by the more vague official moniker of 'integrated resorts'). The first of these, the newly completed **Resorts World Sentosa** (www.rwsentosa.com) on Sentosa Island, features extravagant attractions such as a Universal Studios theme park, the world's largest aquarium, museums, fancy hotels and, of course, casinos, all under one umbrella.

Massive though Resorts World Sentosa is, it's dwarfed by the second of Singapore's integrated resorts at **Marina Bay** (www.marinabaysands.com), which, though not open at the time of this writing, is already casting a huge shadow (literally and figuratively) over Singapore.

Primarily targeted at affluent tourists and the high-rolling super-rich, the resorts form the keystone of the city's bid to plant its flag more aggressively on the world tourism map and become a destination in its own right, rather than a place people pass through on their way to somewhere else.

The decision to build the casinos, coming from a country well known for its strict official morals, raised a few eyebrows at home and abroad, and there was vocal domestic opposition from certain quarters, principally concerned about the potential effect of casinos and their attendant ills of prostitution and crime on Singapore's carefully nurtured social order (though in fact thousands of Singaporeans already go on 'gambling cruises' and pile across to Batam and Genting Highlands for betting orgies).

In response, the resort owners have pledged to impose entrance fees for Singaporeans using the casinos, a move designed to discourage low-income locals, while counselling services for problem gamblers have been loudly trumpeted as a deterrent measure.

ENTERTAINMENT

Once derided as 'Singabore', the Lion City has taken a serious look at the subject of fun (to paraphrase one government minister) and seen that it is good. The results of this nightlife makeover have been mixed, but largely successful, and Singapore has earned itself a solid regional reputation for partying.

Zouk (p81), so long the city's flagship nightclub, now has serious competition cropping up all over Singapore, including entertainment precincts like Clarke Quay and the converted St James Power Station (p134). Periodic beach parties on Sentosa (though nowhere near as wild as their Thai counterparts) have also attracted people from around the region.

The atmosphere is boozy, hedonistic and skimpily dressed, and the official message is that Singapore is Cool, Hip and Happening.

The farcical battles of the past, which once saw the legality of bar-top dancing debated at the highest political levels, have not been entirely consigned to history, however. Though not as gay-friendly as Taipei or Bangkok (the Nation and SnowBall gay parties were shut down, after the government said they were contributing to a rise in HIV infections), Singapore is still pretty tolerant on a social level.

Singapore's place on Asia's flesh-trade map still seems assured, though. While the past two years have seen massive crackdowns on prostitution across town in Geylang (turning this once-notorious hotbed of vice into a slightly less obvious hotbed of vice), thousands of illegal prostitutes at Orchard Towers still operate with limited harassment.

SPORTS

There is scarcely a field of human endeavour for which Singapore does not want to make itself a 'hub', and sport is no exception. The city's aggressive (some would say borderline manic) attempts to sell itself to the world scored a massive boost when it was picked to host a Formula 1 race in September 2008 (see www.singaporegp.sg), sending the local media spin machine into overdrive. Not only that, it won approval to host the first ever F1 night race – no doubt to the vast relief of the drivers and spectators able to avoid the stifling heat of the day.

Since then, the F1 race has become a regular event in Singapore, bringing to a close Singapore's longstanding, Lee Kuan Yew–imposed opposition to motor sport.

Singapore's other sporting endeavours include hosting the 2010 Youth Olympics. Hand in hand with that bid is the development of a modern sports complex on the site of the old and somewhat embarrassingly decrepit National Stadium in Kallang, which was demolished in 2007. The new complex, incomplete at the time of this writing, will feature new stadiums, an aquatic centre and water-sports facility.

The wholesale development of Marina Bay – driven in part by a growing population's thirst for resources (Singapore imports most of its water from Malaysia) – has turned that area into a water-sports centre, protected from the vagaries of the tide by a newly built dam. Branded as a family leisure spot, the dam (dubbed Marina Barrage) is a popular spot with picnickers and photographers looking for a great view of the ever-evolving city skyline.

THE ARTS

Seen alongside the achievements of somewhere comparable, such as Hong Kong, Singapore's endeavours often seem rather bereft. Local painters and sculptors are largely anonymous, writers count publishing runs in the hundreds or low thousands, local movies rarely, if ever, reach large global audiences and theatre companies struggle with a lack of funds, short seasons and small audiences.

However, the city's artistic heart does beat, though faintly. The opening of the world-class Esplanade (p67) was a huge boost to the local arts scene (though small theatre groups might grumble that it swallowed up too much government money). The Singapore Symphony Orchestra and Singapore Chinese Orchestra perform regularly, while March sees the annual Mosaic Music Festival, featuring international acts in everything from hip-hop to jazz to indie bands. There are also periodic outdoor concerts and music festivals at Fort Canning Park, which has hosted the likes of Jet, Incubus and even Black Sabbath.

Theatre and literature struggles. Though the Esplanade manages to attract luminaries such as the Royal Shakespeare Company for brief stints, local groups like Necessary Stage and Wild!Rice often stage productions with quality that veers wildly from the inspired to the mediocre. Furthermore, local audiences are far more likely to shell out money to see well-known international productions instead of supporting local groups.

In addition, theatre groups and artists, both local and foreign, still have to contend with censors, who block gratuitous sexual or religious content, and come down hard on any overt or implied criticism of the government. For example, two locally produced documentaries – on opposition figures JB Jeyaretnam and Chee Soon Juan – have been banned from local film festivals and their directors threatened with legal action.

If Singapore was once a caterpillar, flawlessly functional but uninspiring, it's now a butterfly, albeit one halfway out of its cocoon. Always a great place to eat, drink, dance and play, it's now shedding its conservatism in a big way and becoming one of Asia's cultural capitals.

There is no lack of places to drink and party (p163) in Singapore

ACCOMMODATION

Thanks to a recent boom in boutique and budget hotels, Singapore now has accommodation to suit all tastes and credit-card limits, from $20 dorm beds in Little India to the $1000-plus rooms at the Raffles Hotel, though average room rates have shot up in recent years. With a steady stream of visitors, there is no such thing as a low and high season in Singapore, but it's always advisable to book ahead, particularly if there's a big event in the city. If you're visiting during the annual Formula 1 Grand Prix event you'd be well advised to book months in advance.

During big festivals such as Chinese New Year and Deepavali, booking hotels in Chinatown or Little India will put you at the centre of the festivities, while during National Day, in August, or Chingay, in February, hotels such as the towering cylindrical **Swissôtel**, the **Stamford** (www.singapore-stamford .swissotel.com), historical **Fullerton** (www.fullertonhotel.com) or sexy **Ritz-Carlton** (www.ritzcarlton.com/hotels/singapore) will give you bird's-eye views of the fireworks and the festivities.

For discount deals, check out (you guessed it) www.lonelyplanet .com, but also the plethora of online booking services including www .asiarooms.com or www.singaporehotels.com.

Singapore is a compact city with excellent public transport, so your choice of location is not crucial, but it's worth picking carefully. Shopaholics will prefer to be in the thick of the Orchard Rd action rather than lugging bags home every evening: the five-star functionality of the **Marriott** (www.singaporemarriott.com) or **Meritus Mandarin** (www.meritus-hotels.com) puts you right on top of the malls, while the historic **Goodwood Park** (www.

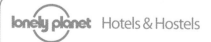

Need a place to stay? Find and book it at lonelyplanet.com. Over 60 properties are featured for Singapore – each personally visited, thoroughly reviewed and happily recommended by a Lonely Planet author. From hostels to high-end hotels, we've hunted out the places that will bring you unique and special experiences. Read independent reviews by authors and other travellers, and get practical information including amenities, maps and photos. Then reserve your room simply and securely via Hotels & Hostels – our online booking service. It's all at lonelyplanet.com/hotels.

goodwoodparkhotel.com) offers a little more ambience. Staying at the **YMCA** (www.ymcaih.com.sg), **SHA Villa** (www.sha.org.sg) or boutique backpacker retreat at **Hangout@Mt.Emily** (www.hangouthotels.com) will save you a little more money to pour into the shops.

Staying in more characterful Chinatown among the narrow lanes, restored shophouses and hawker centres will put you more in touch with the 'real' Singapore. Boutique hotels are the best options. The eccentric gothic **Scarlet Hotel** (www.thescarlethotel.com) might not suit everyone's taste, but the rooftop bar-restaurant views will melt your cynicism. Equally, almost painfully, hip are the **New Majestic Hotel** (www.newmajestichotel.com), whose rooms are individually designed by local artists, and **Hotel 1929** (www.hotel1929.com), where the rooms are the size of cupboards – very fashionable cupboards, though. More traditional shophouse restorations, where you won't feel quite so uncomfortable coming down to breakfast in tracksuit pants, are the **Berjaya Duxton** (www.berjayaresorts.com) or the somewhat more homey **Chinatown** (www.chinatownhotel.com).

Little India specialises in forgettable two- and three-star accommodation, but the restored shophouse strip of the **Perak Hotel** (www.peraklodge.com) is a gem, while the **Inn Crowd** (www.the-inncrowd.com) has installed itself as a firm backpacker favourite.

The opening of Sentosa's Resorts World brings four new choices for visitors looking to stay on Singapore's resort island, all operated under the **Resort World Umbrella** (www.rwsentosa.com). Other spots to stay on Sentosa are the **Sentosa** (www.thesentosa.com), a beautiful, elegant hotel with a priceless clifftop location, and the **Amara Sanctuary** (www.amarasanctuary.com), housed in a former barracks. The ageing **Rasa Sentosa** (www.shangri-la.com) is still the best spot for families and boasts magnificent views.

BEST ON A BUDGET

> Betel Box (www.betelbox.com)
> Hangout@Mt Emily (www.hangouthotels.com)
> Sleepy Sam's (www.sleepysams.com)
> Summer Tavern (www.summertavern.com)
> The Inn Crowd (www.the-inncrowd.com)

BEST BOUTIQUE HOTELS

> Albert Court Hotel (www.albertcourt.com.sg)
> Berjaya Duxton (www.berjayaresorts.com)
> Hotel 1929 (www.hotel1929.com)
> New Majestic Hotel (www.newmajestichotel.com)
> Scarlet Hotel (www.thescarlethotel.com)

FOOD

No subject arouses as much Singaporean passion, or is likelier to provoke an argument, than food. As KF Seetoh, writer and publisher of the *Makansutra* street-food bible, said: 'In Singapore, everyone is a food guide.' Seriously, it would be easier to win a consensus on climate change at the UN than it would be to find two Singaporeans who agree on the best place to eat something. All this bickering means one thing: there's an awful lot of good food out there. Singapore makes a convincing case for being the food capital of Asia. Whether or not that's true, eating is one of the greatest pleasures of this city and anyone who even dares set foot in an American junk-food chain here should be deported immediately and forbidden from returning.

For local food, there is no better place to go than the hawker centres (there are subtle distinctions between hawker centres, food centres, food courts, coffee shops – but for brevity's sake we'll call any collection of stalls a hawker centre). These bustling agglomerations of Chinese, Indian, Malay and bastardised Western cuisines are the happiest consequence of Singapore's cultural stew. They are everywhere – in every shopping mall, on every street, in the public housing blocks, in the dingiest lane – and many are now embellished with Japanese, Korean, Thai and other regional cuisines.

In the perfect world, to visit one famous tourist-friendly hawker centre – be it the overenthusiastically developed Lau Pa Sat (p58), Maxwell Rd (59) or Newton Circus (p46) – would be enough to sample the best of everything. In reality, it's a fluid scene that's very hard to keep track of. Great stalls come and go, move to new locations or (more rarely) just disappear. There's no guarantee that great *char kway teow* you had on your last visit will be there next time. So put your trust in the recommendation of your hotel receptionist or taxi driver and plunge into somewhere new. Websites like **Makansutra** (www.makansutra.com) and **Hungry Go Where** (www.hungrygowhere.com) are excellent resources for anyone serious about exploring hawker centres and stalls – or Singapore cuisine in general – in all their glory.

Be prepared though, sampling the best Singapore hawkers will at some point entail a visit to Geylang, the sleazy red-light district that doubles as the city's street-food capital, and where few Western tourists tread.

For those who prefer to go it alone, arriving at your first centre can be confusing (consult our guide, p59), but spotting the flavour of the month is simple. For many of us, the sight of a queue is an invitation to go elsewhere. For Singaporeans a long queue is like a homing beacon. They will happily stand for half an hour to get a popular dish, even if there's a perfectly delicious but less-busy alternative next door. That's what we call devotion.

While hawker food is Singapore's pride and joy, the city has a huge and fine collection of top restaurants. Excellent Italian and French restaurants abound, particular around the Chinatown area and in Holland Village. Japanese expats have colonised the excellent Cuppage Plaza eateries (and you know they can't be wrong), while homesick Thais head for the seedy surrounds, but superb food, at Golden Mile Complex (p87).

Self-caterers should head for supermarkets such as **Carrefour** (www.carrefour.com.sg) and **Marketplace** (www.coldstorage.com.sg), both of which have superb produce, while speciality shops such as Jones the Grocer (p121) keep the well-heeled supplied with infused oils and expensive cheeses.

BEST TOURIST-FREE HAWKER CENTRES
> Changi Village Hawker Centre (p114)
> Dunman Rd Food Centre (p107)
> Hong Lim Complex (p58)
> Maxwell Rd Hawker Centre (p59)
> Old Airport Rd Food Centre (p110)

BEST STREETS FOR FOOD CRAWL
> Club St
> Geylang Rd
> Joo Chiat Rd/Joo Chiat Pl
> Race Course Rd
> Serangoon Rd

BEST FOR A CANDLELIT EUROPEAN DINNER
> 2am Desert Bar (p122)
> Au Jardin Les Amis (p123)
> L'Angelus (p58)
> Senso (p61)
> The Cliff (p100)

BEST FOR A FANCY CHINESE FEAST
> Guan Hoe Soon (p107)
> Lei Garden (p74)
> My Humble House (p75)
> Peach Garden (p60)
> Shang Palace (p46)

SHOPPING

Singapore's reputation as a cheap shopping destination, like its reputation for dullness, has more to do with its past than its present. For a long time, the likes of Bangkok, Kuala Lumpur and to some extent Hong Kong have eclipsed it for bargains, but Singapore still holds an edge in terms of convenience, while bargains can still be had on some clothing, watches, computer and electrical equipment and Asian antiques.

The Great Singapore Sale, held annually in June, is a good time for cut-price shopping, though the best deals are usually snapped up early. Though bargaining is possible in many places, visitors from other parts of Asia can find that freedom from the exhausting process of haggling comes as a blessed relief, especially on extended shopping excursions through the Grand Canyon of malls that line Orchard Rd (see boxed text, p42).

Get off Orchard Rd and there are many interesting finds to reward the adventurous. Little India (p86) is lined with gold, perfumes, cheap fabrics, spices and handicrafts. Book-ending Little India are the notorious edifices of bargain IT mall Sim Lim Sq (p89) and the 24-hour department store Mustafa Centre (p89), which is an experience in itself.

Down in the Arab Quarter are more fabric, basket- and caneware shops, more jewellery, the hip boutiques of Haji Lane (see boxed text, p87) and the collection of art, handicraft and knick-knack shops on pedestrianised Bussorah St (see boxed text, p87). Nearby, the Bugis St Market is not a patch on the sleaze pit of old, but is a good hunting ground for cheap clothes and knock-offs.

Ignore the tourist stalls of Pagoda and Trengganu Sts in Chinatown. There are some real bargains to be found elsewhere in the area – particularly Asian art and artefacts, though many of the antiques are fake. For a department-store experience with a difference, amble through the five floors of Yue Hwa Chinese Products (p55).

A better place for art and antique hunting is the yuppie ghetto of Dempsey Rd (though the shops predate the area's yuppification), or the gloomy corridors of Tanglin Shopping Centre (not to be confused with Tanglin Mall, stomping ground of the Expatriate Wife).

BEST FOR THE UNEXPECTED FIND
> Bussorah St (boxed text, p87)
> Bugis St Market (p87)
> Far East Plaza (boxed text, p43)
> Haji Lane (boxed text, p87)
> Serangoon Rd and side streets

BEST FOR DESIGNER LABELS
> Ngee Ann City (boxed text, p42)
> Ion Orchard Mall (p39)
> Paragon (boxed text, p42)
> Raffles City (Map pp68–9, F3)
> Tanglin Mall (boxed text, p42)

BEST OFFBEAT MALLS
> Far East Plaza (boxed text, p43)
> Holland Rd Shopping Centre (Map pp118–19, D4)
> Tanglin Shopping Centre (boxed text, p42)
> The Heeren (boxed text, p43)
> Vivocity (boxed text, p132)

BEST STREET MARKETS
> Bugis St Market (p87)
> Sungei Rd Thieves Market (p90)

SINGAPORE FOR KIDS

Singapore offers a plethora of options for children of all ages and inclinations. For a break from the heat, kids will love Wild Wild Wet water park (p113), best visited on weekdays (though at weekends it can be combined with Escape Theme Park (p113) next door).

Sentosa is home to the new Universal Studios theme park (p103), as well as smaller attractions such as the Luge (p103), the Flying Trapeze (p103) and Cineblast (p98). East Coast Park offers both Ski 360° (p113) – a wakeboarding, kneeboarding and water-skiing park – and miles of pathways that are great for riding or skating on rented bikes or rollerblades.

The Singapore Zoo and Night Safari (see boxed text, p48) are very kid-friendly, as is the Bird Park (p138) over in Jurong, which is also home to the entertainingly educational Science Centre (p140). Next door are the Omni-Theatre (p141), showing IMAX films, and sub-zero Snow City (p142). Kids with an interest in Asian myths and legends should appreciate the statues at colourful Haw Par Villa (p135). Finally, the mountain-bike trails on Pulau Ubin (p114) are definitely thrash-worthy for bigger kids – just make sure you rent a decent bike.

BEST FOR SHEER FUN
> Sentosa Luge (p103)
> Ski 360° (p113)
> Snow City (p142)
> Wild Wild Wet (p113)

BEST EDUCATIONAL DAYS OUT
> Haw Par Villa (p135)
> Jurong Bird Park (p138)
> Night Safari (p48)
> Science Centre Singapore (p140)
> Singapore Zoo (p48)

BARS & CLUBS

With countless bars, pubs and clubs of all descriptions, there's no excuse for a quiet night in. Singapore's rigid zoning policies mean bars and clubs are usually corralled into entertainment zones, which is good for pub crawls, but not so good if you're after a quiet neighbourhood drink.

Along Orchard Rd, the most popular haunt is Emerald Hill (see boxed text, p49), a collection of small, funky shophouse bars (which are all actually owned by the same company). In the Colonial District, an old convent compound has been beautifully, if a little cheekily, converted into the popular CHIJMES entertainment hub (Map pp68–9, E3).

The quays heave at night. Boat Quay draws the bankers and tourists (and the touts that hassle them), so nip one street back to the smaller spots on Circular Rd (Map pp68-9, D6). Redeveloped Clarke Quay (Map pp68-9, D5) has exploded in recent years, turning the whole area into a seething nest of dancing – check the Rupee Room (p78), the Butter Factory (p81) and Cuba Libre (p76). Extroverts will want to hit the Actor's Bar (p75), and introverts might be better suited to the quieter spots further upriver in Robertson Quay.

The CBD falls quiet at night, but there's a pocket of activity in Far East Sq, which hosts the boozy Belgian bar Oosters (p62) and Kazbar (p61). For that neighbourhood drink, head to Club St (Map pp52-3, E3) in Chinatown, the BluJaz Café (p93) in the Arab Quarter, the Prince of Wales (p94) in Little India, or somewhere around Holland Rd or Bukit Timah.

The eight bars/clubs at St James Power Station (see boxed text, p134) complex in the southwest of the city, meanwhile, have emerged as a serious contender for Singapore's hottest nightspot.

BEST FOR DANCING
> Butter Factory (p81)
> Cuba Libre (p76)
> Movida (p134)
> Rupee Room (p78)
> Zouk (p81)

BEST FOR BEER
> Archipelago (p76)
> Brewerkz (p76)
> Oosters (p62)
> Paulaner Brauhaus (p77)
> Red Dot Brewhouse (p126)

FASHION

If asked to sum up Singapore's fashion sense in one phrase, 'smart casual' would be the most accurate. This is no Tokyo – the most adventurous dressers you're likely to see are the occasional, mostly Malay, teen goths, but even they are only conforming to a prescribed look. Singapore has, at least until a recent about-turn, always heavily discouraged individuality, which is strongly reflected in the local dress sense. Polo tees and jeans are all the rage, while teen girls and young women favour tiny denim shorts and miniskirts, often coupled with a singlet and ballet flats. Out in the heartlands, flip-flops (thongs), bermudas and T-shirts is the uniform of choice, while in the city, the sharp-dressed office dude will sport a striped shirt, black trousers, pointy or square-toed shoes and, of course, heavily gelled hair (not forgetting the phone clutched in one hand, or the mobile earpiece).

Despite this glaring absence of the unorthodox and the preoccupation with ubiquitous international designer brands, there are several notable hunting grounds for alternative wear. On Orchard Rd, head for the Heeren (p43) or Far East Plaza (p43), the former for local designers, the latter for cheap chic and the occasionally outlandish. Parco Bugis Junction maintains a small nest of local-designer outlets, while across the road the Bugis St Market (p87) sometimes yields a few surprises.

Top local names such as **Daniel Yam** (www.danielyam.com), **Anthea Chan** (www .perfectinblack.com) and, for the wildly offbeat, **K Mi Huang** (www.w-o-m-b.com) are a match for any international label.

Fashion show at the Paragon (see boxed text, p42) in Orchard Rd

LIVE MUSIC

The live-music scene in Singapore was once pretty dismal, but while there are still few original local bands of note, the situation has improved beyond measure.

Classical buffs are well catered for, with regular performances by the Singapore Symphony Orchestra and Singapore Chinese Orchestra at the Esplanade (p67). Free outdoor concerts are held regularly on Fridays at the Esplanade and periodically on the Symphony Stage in the Botanic Gardens. Tickets for bigger concerts can be had from **Sistic** (www.sistic.com.sg) or **TicketCharge** (www.ticketcharge.com.sg).

Big pop and rock acts occasionally pass through, playing at the Singapore Indoor Stadium or Fort Canning Park (p39), but there are a host of great bands playing residences at places such as St James Power Station (p134), the Arena (p80) and Cuba Libre (p76), while venues such as Crazy Elephant (p78) and the Substation (Map pp68–9, E3) are the pick of the venues for local bands. The Prince of Wales (p94) in Little India regularly hosts decent local and expat outfits, as well as a patchy selection of earnest acoustic strummers (A pint of poetic misery sir? Coming right up). Check www.musicforgood.org for upcoming local concerts and events.

Options for jazz lovers are relatively limited. The best option is Southbridge Jazz @ 7atenine (p78), featuring many of the same musicians from Singapore's first jazz club, Jazz @ Southbridge. At weekends, BluJaz Café (p93) and Harry's Bar (p76) are also decent places for jazz buffs to catch shows. The Bellini Room at St James Power Station (p134) features irresistibly foot-tapping swing bands.

BEST FOR JAZZ
> Bellini Room (p134)
> BluJaz Café (p93)
> Harry's Bar (p76)
> Southbridge Jazz @ 7atenine (p78)

BEST FOR LIVE BANDS
> Crazy Elephant (p78)
> Movida (p134)
> Prince of Wales (p94)
> The Arena (p80)
> Wala Wala (p127)

ARCHITECTURE

Like many cities throughout the world, Singapore went through its own Dark Ages during the '60s and '70s, when the world fell in love with the functional concrete box. The result? The demolishing of much architectural heritage in a wrecking-ball frenzy.

Happily, sense eventually prevailed and there are preserved pockets of Singapore's wonderful architecture, though the concrete-box merchants still have plenty of work building the ubiquitous Housing & Development Board flats. The city's Colonial District is a treasure chest of tropical Palladian design, while Chinatown's remaining historical shophouses around Telok Ayer, Tanjong Pagar and the lanes off South Bridge Rd are heritage protected.

Around Joo Chiat, there are large pockets of traditional Peranakan shophouses – notable for their ornate facades and cool central courtyards.

Opinion is divided (as always) on the new buildings. Most people either love or hate the spiky durian-like Esplanade and the Norman Foster–designed 'spaceship' of the Supreme Court, while the oddly isolated, Gotham-style Parkview Sq puzzles a few. Worth spotting are the IM Pei–designed twin towers of the Gateway, designed to look two-dimensional from whatever angle you see it. For a masterpiece of melded modern and traditional design, visit the National Museum of Singapore (p70) – and check out those swinging chandeliers.

BEST MODERN BUILDINGS
> Esplanade (p67)
> Ion Orchard Mall (p39)
> Parkview Sq (Map pp68–9, G2)
> Singapore Management University (Map pp68–9, F3)
> Supreme Court (Map pp68–9, E5)

BEST OLD BUILDINGS
> Asian Civilisations Museum (p67)
> Fullerton Hotel (Map pp68–9, F6)
> National Museum of Singapore (p70)
> Old Parliament House (The Arts House; Map pp68–9, E5)
> Raffles Hotel (p71)

GREEN SINGAPORE

A tiny island – with 4.5 million people stuffed into it – the mental image first-time visitors often have of Singapore is that of a human anthill, a concrete metropolis entirely given over to flats, industry and money making.

They soon discover otherwise. Quite apart from the huge number of city parks (p168), Singapore boasts wetlands, mangroves and, rather impressively, one of the only two patches of urban primary rainforest in the world, in the form of Bukit Timah Nature Reserve (p117).

The centre of the island is entirely devoted to forests and reservoirs, and the mangroves that once ringed the island are preserved in three main visitable pockets – Sungei Buloh Wetland Reserve (see boxed text, p141), Pasir Ris Park (p112) and Chek Jawa on Pulau Ubin (see boxed text, p114) – which teem with bird life, otters, monitor lizards and even a few crocodiles.

The forests of Bukit Timah and the Central Catchment Nature Reserve (see Walking Tour, p146) are the best places to spot long-tailed macaques, flying lemurs, pythons, lizards and hundreds of bird species.

Singapore is slowly converting to the environmental cause, though a noticeable recent worsening in traffic volume and the slow adoption of recycling must surely threaten its green policies and its generally good air quality. The government produces three-yearly revisions to its 2012 Green Plan, which commits the island to reducing carbon-dioxide emissions, water consumption and air pollution, and improving waste management.

The island cannot control the actions of its neighbours, though, and from June to September the thick, pungent haze drifting from Indonesian plantation fires can send air quality plummeting for weeks on end.

Couple having a picnic at the Singapore Botanic Gardens (p117)

V

PARKS

It's the first thing many visitors notice: the extravagant botanical displays lining the expressway leading from Changi Airport. It isn't just window dressing either. Singapore has some serious greenery.

One of the happier consequences of strict government control has been the creation of hundreds of city and neighbourhood parks. They aren't just vacant patches of land grudgingly cordoned off from eager developers by an apathetic local council either.

Singapore's parks are often masterpieces of design and landscaping, from the tiniest urban oasis such as Telok Ayer Garden (Map pp52–3, F4) to the forests of Kent Ridge Park (p129) and Labrador Nature Reserve (p129) and the large manicured spaces of East Coast Park (see boxed text, p112). Expect to find bicycle paths, unvandalised benches, exercise routes complete with equipment, lily ponds, foot-reflexology paths, bird-watching hides, mangrove walks, restaurants, museums, spice gardens and vegetable patches, dog runs and barbecue pits. A huge network of park connectors enables cyclists and runners to basically circumnavigate the island without encountering a road. Though not 100% finished, it was pretty close to being done at the time of writing.

To enter one of these wonderful places is to believe that, for all the cynicism the Singaporean social experiment arouses, this is a city that has passionately pursued the restorative power of green space in a crowded environment and, just perhaps, has its citizens' welfare at heart.

BEST WATERFRONT PARKS
> East Coast Park (see boxed text, p112)
> Labrador Nature Reserve (p129)
> MacRitchie Reservoir Nature Park (see Walking Tour, p146)
> Pasir Ris Park (p112)

BEST IN THE CITY TO ESCAPE THE CITY
> Fort Canning Park (p39)
> Kent Ridge Park (p129)
> Labrador Nature Reserve (p129)
> Mt Faber Park (p135)
> Telok Ayer Garden (Map pp52–3, F4)

CELLULOID

Singaporeans are avid movie-goers and proudly boast that more movie tickets are sold here per capita than anywhere else in the world. Visitors need to arm themselves with warm clothing and a large reserve of patience, however: Singaporeans love to chat and rustle their snack packets during movies, and the air-con is often so high it'll make your teeth chatter.

Hollywood rules here – the more mainstream the better and in the city centre huge crowds queue up for tickets to the latest blockbuster, romantic comedy or CGI-animals crowd-pleaser. To avoid frustration, booking in advance at **Golden Village** (www.gv.com.sg) lets you skip the queue.

The city's growing sophistication has seen a couple of options emerge for international and alternative movies: Cinema Europa at Golden Village Vivocity (p132) and the hip, luxurious Screening Room (p65) in Chinatown. Once a year, in April, the Singapore International Film Festival (p25) showcases more than a hundred independent movies from all over the world.

Golden Village's Gold Class at Vivocity has waiter service and plush reclining seats, but the higher ticket prices mean the movie had better be worth it.

Singaporean cinema has never quite found a voice or style of its own. Local productions are derivative and vary widely in quality, which, given the island's negligible output, it can scarcely afford (see p185).

BEST CINEMAS TO AVOID

> Cathay Cineleisure Orchard – takes forever to get upstairs
> Eng Wah Toa Payoh – crowd noise
> Lido at Shaw House – long weekend queues, very cold

BEST OFFBEAT AND LUXURY CINEMAS

> Cinema Europa at Vivocity (p132)
> Golden Village's Gold Class at Vivocity (p132)
> The Picturehouse at the Cathay (p42)
> The Screening Room (p65)

MUSEUMS

Singapore is almost embarrassingly well endowed with museums, from the tiny and obscure to the grand and meaty, many of them clustered around the Colonial District.

There's a certain understandable preoccupation with Singapore history, to the point of repetition, and the political overtones sometimes get a little heavy, but by and large they are excellent.

The city's pride and joy is the Asian Civilisations Museum (p67) – they took George W Bush there, and doubtless he revelled in the academic pursuit of foreign cultural understanding. Second in the pecking order is the National Museum of Singapore (p70), magnificently restored and kitted out with an impressive modern annex. The Singapore Art Museum (p71) nearby focuses on the regional art experience, but also houses the works of names such as Rothko.

The anguish of Singapore's WWII experience is marked in several places (see p19). This watershed period in the country's history is covered in depth over several museums and commemorated at several sites: including Fort Siloso on Sentosa, Memories at Bukit Chandu at Kent Ridge Park, Memories at Old Ford Factory in Bukit Timah, as well as at the National Museum and Images of Singapore on Sentosa. The trauma of occupation, and Singapore's tetchy postwar relations with its larger neighbours, have inspired its obsession with security today.

Of the specific cultural museums, the Chinatown Heritage Centre (p51) is the best, followed by its sister Peranakan Museum (p70), which studies the region's mixed Malay-Chinese ethnic community.

MUST NOT MISS
> Asian Civilisations Museum (p67)
> National Museum of Singapore (p70)
> Peranakan Museum (p70)
> Singapore Art Museum (p71)

BEST FOR THE WAR EXPERIENCE
> Changi Memorial & Chapel (p106)
> Fort Siloso (p98)
> Reflections At Bukit Chandu (p132)
> The Battle Box (p39)
> Kranji War Memorial (p177)

GAY & LESBIAN SINGAPORE

Thumping gay clubs, saunas and massage parlours in discreet doorways, lesbians holding hands in the street, drag queens on the TV – hold on, is this really uptight, repressive Singapore?

As with many things in this city, its stance on homosexuality is enigmatic. Male homosexuality is illegal, yet its many gay clubs, bars and saunas – centred on Chinatown – operate openly and largely unmolested by police. Even Lee Kuan Yew, architect of Singapore's official moral code, has made veiled conciliatory noises suggesting the government's antigay stance may be outdated.

Having said that, the government is not going to open the floodgates just yet. Police refused further permits for two highly successful annual gay parties that had attracted regional attention: Nation and SnowBall. The prime minister backed them up, saying Singapore was not ready for the promotion of gay lifestyles.

For the best and latest information and listings, check www.utopia-asia .com, or try local lifestyle site www.trevvy.com (which replaced the banned www.sgboy.com) or regional gay and lesbian site www.fridae.com.

As for lesbians, legally they don't exist, which means the law must be walking around with eyeshades on, because you'd be hard pressed to spend more than a few hours in any street or mall without seeing lesbian couples, often walking hand in hand, sometimes more, and attracting no obvious attention. In fact, there is unlikely to be a city in Asia, perhaps even the world, where lesbians are more visible.

In 2007 the government banned an Xbox game that features a human-alien, all-female kissing scene. Evidently embarrassed by the worldwide headlines the ban generated, the government relented.

SPORTS

Despite the roaringly hot and humid year-round conditions in their city, Singaporeans are keen on outdoor pursuits.

Cyclists can arrange rides with the **ANZA club** (www.anzacycling.com) or the **Cycleworx shop** (www.cycleworx.com). Mountain-bikers can use the Bukit Timah Nature Reserve trail (p117), but there are no bikes for hire there. Pulau Ubin's trails are excellent, and good bikes can be rented right off the boat dock.

Runners can hook up with the approachable **MacRitchie Runners** (www.mr25.org.sg). Endurance sports are very popular and there are regular races, usually at East Coast Park. Check with the **Triathlon Association** (www.triathlonsingapore.org).

Even with space contraints, Singapore has somehow found room for a surprising number of golf courses, but green fees for nonmembers are high, ranging from $90 on less-prestigious courses such as Jurong Country Club to $450 for a weekend round at the championship Serapong course (p103).

Rock climbers will find the Dairy Farm Quarry (frequented by local climbers at weekends) a challenge, while equestrians might be interested in checking out the riding options over at either Horse City (p127) in the west or Gallop Stable (p112) in the east.

Given its oily seas, Singapore isn't great for beach swimming, but if your hotel doesn't have a pool, then public pools, are clean and cheap. Sailors and windsurfers have the choice of several sea sports clubs – see www.water-venture.org.sg for info. Constant Wind (p111) rents sailboards and boats to the public.

For wakeboarders, water skiers and kneeboarders, the Ski 360° (p113) cable-ski lagoon at East Coast Park is a must.

Idyllic Fort Canning Park (p39) is located in the heart of the city

>BACKGROUND

The iconic Asian Civilisations Museum (p67) stands picturesque against the Singapore River

BACKGROUND

HISTORY

Malay legend tells of Sumatran prince Sang Nila Utama sheltering from a storm on the island of Temasek and spotting a lion – a good omen that prompted the prince to found a city there called Singapura (Lion City). It is of course highly unlikely that lions ever roamed the island's forests, but it's somehow an appropriate tale for a city so adept at creating mythologies.

Actual records of Singapore's early history are sketchy. Originally it was an insignificant port squeezed between muscular neighbours Sumatra and Melaka, and there are records of Chinese traders visiting the island, which appeared on Chinese maps as Pu-Luo-Chong as far back as AD 300.

Singapore's official history begins in 1819 with the arrival of Sir Stamford Raffles, who was declared Singapore's founder in the 1970s in order to 'neutrally' settle rival claims by local Malays and Chinese. With no claims to indigenous rights, Singapore has been free to do as it pleases with its land.

COLONIAL CONQUEST

In the late 18th century Britain began looking for a harbour in the Strait of Melaka that would usurp its Portuguese and Dutch competitors and secure its trade routes between China, India and the Malay world.

Young Stamford Raffles arrived in Singapore in 1819 to find the Johor empire divided, with two contenders for the sultanship. The Dutch favoured one candidate, so Raffles backed the rival contender Hussein and proclaimed him sultan, clinching the deal by signing a treaty with an eminent *temenggong* (senior judge). This exchange ended with the 1824 cash buyout of Hussein and the judge, transferring Singapore's ownership to the British East India Company. The last sultan, Ali Iskander Shah, was given an *istana* (palace) in Kampong Glam that still stands there today, though the family moved out in 1999 and the building now houses the Malay Heritage Centre.

Raffles laid down the initial plans for the development of the free-trade port, which had attracted thousands of immigrant traders and merchants. Spotting the potential for conflict, Raffles delineated ethnic districts in his city plans that remain today. The streets of Chinatown,

Little India, the Arab Quarter and the Colonial District are just as Raffles drew them nearly 200 years ago.

The man charged with turning these plans into physical reality was town surveyor George Drumgoole Coleman, a talented Irishman who was responsible for the city's central road network and many of its finest buildings. He skilfully adapted the Palladian style to fit the tropical climate, designing buildings such as Caldwell House in CHIJMES (now a pleasant spot for an evening beer), Old Parliament House, Armenian Church and St Andrew's Cathedral, as well as Thian Hock Keng Temple and the Hajjah Fatimah Mosque.

THE EARLY COLONY

Singapore was soon teeming with Chinese immigrants. Back in 1879, European traveller Isabella Bird noted the 'resistless, overpowering, astonishing Chinese element, which is gradually turning Singapore into a Chinese city!'

Many of these Chinese, mostly from China's southern provinces, landed at the Thian Hock Keng Temple in Chinatown (which was on the seashore at that time), then were quickly absorbed into their respective communities by the clan societies, whose headquarters once lined Club St, where a few remain.

The indolence and heat-induced torpor Bird described in other parts of Asia and the Pacific were entirely absent from early Singapore. From the beginning it was dynamic and driven, its population inspired into frenzied activity by the lure of fortune. The British forged good trading relations with the Straits-born Chinese-Malays, known as Peranakans, who found an identity in the Union Jack, British law and citizenship.

Conditions, except for the British ensconced in their breezy colonial villas, were tough. A visit to the Chinatown Heritage Centre (p51) provides an accurate insight into life in that neighbourhood, riddled as it was with bad sanitation, disease, British Empire–sponsored opium addiction, gang warfare and prostitution. Violence was common and policing minimal.

THE BELLY OF THE CARP

During the early boom years of Singapore, Chinese traders favoured Boat Quay because at that point the river was shaped like the belly of the carp, which is an auspicious symbol for business in Chinese belief. In this case, they were often right.

In 1887 the interracial tensions Raffles had meant to forestall with his segregated town plan led to riots, not for the last time.

But the city was booming. Along the Singapore River, the sloping tiled roofs where you can now sit for a few drinks and a nice meal once sheltered the *towkays* (businessmen) who set up trading houses along the bank for goods such as rubber, tin, rice, coffee and steel, turning the area into the economic engine room of the city. The bumboats that ferry tourists up and down the river were in the mid- to late 1800s so tightly jammed around Boat Quay you could almost have crossed the river by stepping between them.

By the 1930s and early 1940s the rumblings of international politics began to filter into the city. The Indian independence movement and communist struggles in China captured Singapore's imagination, causing the British a few palpitations. However, whatever winds of change were rustling Singapore society were soon blown away by the storm of WWII.

WWII & THE JAPANESE INVASION

Some historians label the Japanese occupation of Singapore as the key moment in the decline of the British Empire, the moment that tore apart the myth of British military might on an island once viewed as an impregnable fortress.

The impact of the occupation on the collective memory of this island cannot be underestimated. Just look at the sheer number of museums and memorials (p170) devoted to the memory and study of the invasion.

General Yamashita Tomoyuki pushed his thinly stretched army into the northwest of Singapore on 15 February 1942. Around 140,000 Australian, New Zealand, British and oft-overlooked Indian, Dutch and Malay troops were killed or imprisoned in the invasion.

If the invasion was a humiliation for the British Empire, it was a disaster for many of those who lived through it. The Allied soldiers were herded into the horrors of the Changi POW camp or shipped off to the worse fate of building the Death Railway in Thailand.

Singaporean Chinese paid an equally heavy price. Thousands of Chinese (Singapore claims 50,000; Japan says 6000) were targeted for torture and mass execution at Sentosa and Changi Beach, where a memorial marks the spot of the slaughter.

Japanese rule was harsh in Singapore, temporarily renamed Syonan (Light of the South). Malays and Indians were subject to systematic

THE KRANJI WAR MEMORIAL

The Allied **war cemetery** (☎ 6269 6158; 9 Woodlands Rd; admission free; ☯ 7am-6pm; M Kranji MRT, 🚍 170) contains around 4000 graves and memorial walls bearing the inscribed names of 24,346 people whose bodies were never recovered. There are registers listing the dead by the memorial walls and visitors books at the entrance. Like all war cemeteries, it's a distressing sight. The one heart-warming aspect of the place is the team of diligent groundsmen that keeps the place in an immaculate state.

abuse. Inflation skyrocketed; food, medicines and other essentials became scarce, and starvation ensued.

When the war ended with the atomic bombing and Japan's surrender on 14 August 1945, Singapore was passed back into British control. Despite an official apology in 1991 and generous monetary loans, Singapore has never forgotten the Japanese, a fact you only have to visit somewhere like Reflections at Bukit Chandu (p132) to witness.

POSTWAR ALIENATION

The British were welcomed back to Singapore but their right (and ability) to rule was now in seriously in question. Postwar poverty, unemployment and nationalist sentiment provided a groundswell of support for communism, and Singapore moved slowly towards self-government.

By the early 1950s the 'communist threat' had waned but left-wing activity was still on the upswing. One of the rising stars of this era was Lee Kuan Yew, a third-generation Straits-born Chinese who had studied law at Cambridge. The socialist People's Action Party (PAP) was founded in 1954 with Lee as secretary-general.

Under arrangements for internal self-government, PAP won a majority of seats in the new Legislative Assembly in 1959, and Lee Kuan Yew became the first Singapore prime minister – a title he held for the next 31 years.

INDEPENDENT SINGAPORE

By the early 1960s Britain had devised a way to withdraw regional colonial rule by creating the new state of Malaysia, uniting Malaya with Sabah, Sarawak and Singapore. In 1965 Singapore was expelled, largely due to Malay fears of Chinese dominance. Singapore reluctantly

SIR STAMFORD RAFFLES

Even viewed from today's anticolonial perspective, Sir Stamford Raffles was an extraordinary individual. Only 45 when he died of a probable brain tumour, the man who started as a humble clerk was an accomplished naturalist, cultural scholar, enlightened colonial governor, Malay speaker, founder of the London Zoo and the visionary who effectively created the city of Singapore. But he ended his life in frustration and unhappiness, having lost four of his five children and having the East India Company refuse his pension. The vicar who buried Raffles had interests in slave plantations and refused him a memorial stone, because he objected to Raffles' friendship with abolitionist William Wilberforce. Six years after his death, his accomplishments were recognised with a statue in Westminster Abbey.

struck out on its own and vigorously survived. Despite having no natural resources, under Lee Kuan Yew it quickly entrenched itself as a manufacturing, trading and financial centre, transforming itself into an economic powerhouse.

In the process, Lee embarked on an experiment in social engineering that has been famous and infamous in equal measure, attracting admiration from some quarters (foreign governments eager to replicate its level of control reportedly send frequent delegations to study the 'Singapore system') and hostility from others.

There have been strict laws imposed on Singapore's population (the chewing gum ban and jaywalking laws being the most well-known, but by no means the most severe) and political opposition has been ruthlessly quashed.

Lee stepped down in 1990, handing over to Goh Chok Tong, an erudite, avuncular but equally tough figure sometimes unfairly dismissed as a place-holder for Lee Kuan Yew's oldest son, Lee Hsien Loong, who became PM in 2004.

Lee the Younger faces challenges perhaps as tough as those that greeted his father in 1965. Maintaining Singapore's strength involves remodelling itself as a global city and a hub for anything and everything: transport, high finance, IT, higher education, medical travel, digital media, the arts, conferences, tourism, biomedical engineering. For this, it needs to import thousands more professionals and labourers, but in the process maintain the traditional social order and values that bind the island's society. Singapore is a city in flux. It's fascinating to watch it in process – and it will be fascinating to see where it goes.

LIFE AS A SINGAPOREAN

Being part of the Singapore miracle has bestowed upon many of the island's residents a level of economic prosperity and freedom their grandparents, and even parents, could never have imagined. They enjoy decent education, health care, infrastructure, low levels of crime, clean water, plentiful food and freedom to travel – a modern lifestyle millions of citizens in countries neighbouring Singapore aspire to, but will struggle to achieve in this generation.

The average Singaporean will live in a privately owned, government-built unit known as a Housing & Development Board (HDB) flat, which will have been purchased using money from their compulsory government savings account, known as the CPF. Life usually involves early starts and long hours of work that helps pay off hefty home and possibly car loans – Singapore has the costliest cars in the world – though the domestic load is often lightened by many with the employment of a live-in maid from Indonesia or the Philippines.

Children are pushed hard from a young age and spend long hours at school, and are often thrust into extracurricular activities in the manic rush for places at top schools and universities.

Each of the HDB 'towns' cram in many thousands of families, and the sense of community that once thrived in the old kampong (villages), which were torn down to make way for them, has been harder to replicate. As a Singaporean you are bombarded with efforts to forge a strong national and racial identity, and persistently badgered by official campaigns – Speak Good English! Speak Mandarin! Be More Considerate! Be Spontaneous! Be More Careful! Drive Courteously! A well-oiled media spin machine churns out whatever stories are deemed necessary to reinforce the political and social agenda.

Local councils try to forge community bonds through the organisation of regular events at the 'void decks' (empty areas beneath blocks of flats) or community centres, where you'll often see large congregations of people tucking into meals and being entertained by singers on temporary stages.

To enjoy this level of comfort, Singaporeans have been required to enter into a social contract: namely, the government delivers prosperity and security to them and, in return, they don't rock the boat. The explicit message spun to every Singaporean, particularly through the country's docile media, is that the country's prosperity depends entirely on the maintenance of the political status quo.

Privately many people – especially those battling rising poverty, a growing income gap and a rapidly increasing cost of living – complain bitterly about the situation, but few dare do much else, because the stories of what has happened to those who have openly challenged the political or social order are ingrained in the national consciousness: lawsuits, bankruptcy, jail, ruin. And in reality, deep down even those who grumble often support the system, because the alternatives are presented as all too frightening.

Though many long-term residents speak of a subtle climate of fear, most short-term visitors will find Singaporeans on the whole to be friendly, helpful and engaging, often diffident but often ready for a good laugh.

It is true, though, that years of well-meaning multicultural social engineering seems to have engendered an acute preoccupation with questions of race and identity, and don't be surprised if some aspect of your behaviour is interpreted not as a personal characteristic, but as the indelible product of your racial identity. The fatal race riots that fractured the city in the '60s may be far in the past, but they are kept fresh in the political memory, and the message of multiculturalism and religious plurality is continually reinforced through the local councils, annual festivals and the media.

Beneath the surface, remnants of racial enmity simmer, but economic success and harsh punishments for those who voice racist views has kept a lid on them. Even so, levels of hostility towards foreigners, whether it's the *ang moh* (Westerners) or *bangla* (labourers from the Indian subcontinent), exist, though it's more often openly expressed as ridicule rather than outright dislike.

Food and football are by far the best ways to dip a toe into Singaporean culture. Food is a local passion, an indispensable part of a happy life, and Singaporeans devote hours to eating, thinking about eating, or talking about where to eat. In a city preoccupied with status and hierarchy, food is the great social leveller – the love of eating will see managing directors pull up plastic chairs next to tables of foreign construction workers (though proximity does not translate as interaction). Choose a local dish, ask someone where is the best place to find it and, presto, you have a conversation.

Anyone with an interest in football – or more specifically English Premier League football – will also find instant common ground with most Singaporean males, and many females, who have adopted club partisanship with a level of passionate devotion that rivals the English (or Thais, or Malaysians, or Chinese!). Coffee shops and pubs are packed out for games, though of course physical violence between rival fans is almost unheard of.

Beneath all the modernity and apparent Westernisation, strict Confucian family ideals still hold sway. Though there are signs these ideals are in decline, filial piety for Chinese Singaporeans is still an overarching philosophy, which sees many people living in extended families, or at least living close to their parents. It is explicitly expected that citizens extend the same level of self-sacrifice to the nation.

One obvious manifestation of this principle is national service. All Singaporean men live under the constant shadow (or beam of sunshine, depending on who you talk to) of military service. As well as their compulsory two years of duty, all males are required to be on standby and most have to do a stint for a couple of weeks a year.

GOVERNMENT & POLITICS

Politics in Singapore is both everywhere and nowhere. Everywhere, in the sense that, with the increasingly significant exception of the web pages that pop up on the computer screens of Singapore's citizens, everything you see, read and hear has at some point felt the guiding hand of government upon it. But it's nowhere in that the ebb and flow of conflicting opinions and ideas in a public forum is almost non-existent.

The People's Action Party has held power in Singapore since 1959 and has been virtually the sole political force since 1965, when the island was kicked out of the Malay Federation after an uneasy alliance forged in 1963. Prime Minister Lee Kuan Yew famously cried on TV the day Singapore was left to fend for itself, but he's shed few tears since.

The white-clad party he led with steely paternalism is still in control to this day. Opposition voices like JB Jeyaretnam, Francis Seow and Chee Soon Juan have been removed from the political process via lawsuits and financial ruin. (According to Singapore law, bankrupted citizens aren't allowed to run for election.) Many Singaporeans find persuasive the argument that a successful government doesn't need challenging, while others believe that the government – precisely because of its success – ought to be more tolerant of criticism.

UNCLE HARRY
While the nascent Singapore city was created by the vision of Sir Stamford Raffles, modern Singapore is undoubtedly the vision of Lee Kuan Yew. A Straits-born Chinese known as Harry Lee, he was educated at the prestigious Raffles Institution and then in law at Cambridge University. He was, he said, raised to be 'the equal of any Englishman'. Despite resigning as PM in 1990, he still oversees and directs policy in his role as Minister Mentor, and once said: 'Even if you are going to lower me into the grave and I feel that something is wrong, I'll get up.'

Though voting in Singapore is mandatory, elections are carefully managed, with rallies, speeches and posters (in short, all the trappings of a parliamentary democracy). But the system, many argue, is engineered to produce only one result – a win for the ruling party.

Even so, the PAP only won 66% of the vote at the last election in 2006, a fall of nearly 9% from the previous election, though they still took 82 of parliament's 84 seats. For the first time since 1988, the PAP was not automatically returned to power on nomination day via uncontested seats. The constituencies of Hougang and Potong Pasir, despite heavy inducements from the PAP in the form of promised HDB upgrading projects, remained defiantly in opposition hands.

The opposition Worker's Party attracted huge crowds to its rallies before the poll, filling two sports stadiums, but the stories of these rallies never appeared in the local press.

Which brings us to the internet. The PAP is slowly waking up to the realities of the online world, but its reactions to events often betray a mindset stuck in the days when most information channels could be managed. Photos of those 2006 Worker's Party rallies were up on the internet within hours, just one example of how the net has given birth to a new era of political discussion and a forum for dissent in Singapore.

Visit http://singabloodypore.rsfblog.org and see the sheer number of links to other political blogs. Some of them are wild rants, others are considered, thoughtful analyses.

Whether or not this is indicative of any fundamental grassroots change remains to be seen. As long as Singapore remains prosperous, the PAP is likely to remain politically secure, but as that prosperity is leaving an ever-growing local underclass behind, even that may not be taken for granted.

ENVIRONMENT

Sir Stamford Raffles would hardly recognise it. There are few reminders now of the Singapore of old – thickly forested, ringed with swampy mangrove, patrolled by snakes and tigers and highly malarial. The only spots where it's still possible to see Singapore's indigenous environment are Pulau Ubin (see boxed text, p114), Bukit Timah (p117) and the Sungei Buloh Wetland Reserve (p141). The rest of the island has been stripped, cleaned, moulded, flattened and enlarged to squeeze in people, roads and industries.

The effect of all this on the island's ecology has naturally been dramatic. The last tiger was shot in the 1930s (some place this event in Choa Chu Kang in the west of the island, others at the Raffles Hotel). Other wildlife remains in the forests that dominate the centre of the island: macaques, monitor lizards, flying lemurs, pythons, the occasional cobra and anteater, 364 bird species and around 935 kinds of insect, though new ones continue to be discovered.

Under the sea, land reclamation, the constant flow of container vessels and massive heavy industry has combined to destroy much of the country's marine ecosystem. Though pockets of reef remain offshore from islands such as St John's, the 'forests of coral' described by Isabella Bird in 1879 are long gone.

Singapore's flora is more prodigious. One naturalist estimated that there were more plant varieties in Singapore than in the whole of North America, despite the fact that only a tiny percentage of the original forest and mangrove cover remains.

HANDS OFF OUR SAND

In January 2007 the Indonesian government sprung a surprise when it announced it was banning exports of sand to Singapore. This sand, used for Singapore's massive land-reclamation projects and construction industry, was suddenly in short supply, sparking huge price increases and palpitations in high office. Officially, Indonesia said the ban had been enacted to protect the country's environment, but people familiar with Indonesia's somewhat patchy environmental record said it was more likely a tool to pressure Singapore to sign an extradition treaty that Indonesia hoped would help it recover billions of dollars in embezzled Indonesian funds allegedly secreted into Singapore's financial system. Negotiations did begin over an extradition treaty, but the ban remains in place. Besides, sand extraction had already decimated large parts of the Riau archipelago's marine ecosystem, begging the question: why now?

FURTHER READING

The wealth of historical and political literature on Singapore is a testament not only to the importance of its strategic role, but the fascination this tiny and formerly seedy port city inspired, particularly among the Europeans, who account for the vast majority of historical and fictional writing. Local fiction has always been a little thin on the ground, but there has been a recent resurgence in local writing. Many of the following will be available in Kinokuniya (p39), Borders or the academic **Select Books** (p42; www.selectbooks.com.sg), and though some are out of print (or banned) they are available secondhand through Amazon.

Travellers' Singapore, a collection of accounts taking in a broad sweep from the early 1800s to 1942, and the similar *Travellers' Tales of Old Singapore* are the most entertaining way to get an overview of the island's past.

Raffles, by Maurice Collis, is by far the best biography of the great scholar and statesman, while the most damning account of the fall of the island to the Japanese in 1942 is *Singapore: The Pregnable Fortress* by Peter Elphick.

It isn't quite the *Little Red Book* – it's hardly little, for one thing – but a copy of Lee Kuan Yew's *Singapore Story* is obligatory for anyone wanting to understand not only how the Singapore miracle came about, but also the thinking of the man who masterminded it.

For a glimpse into the darker side of that same miracle, *Lee's Law,* by Chris Lydgate, offers a disturbing account of the rise and systematic destruction of Singapore's most famous dissenter, lawyer and opposition member JB Jeyaretnam. James Minchin's *No Man Is An Island* presents a broad critical study of Lee Kuan Yew. Another lawyer, former Law Society president, Francis Seow, has penned two similar books: *To Catch A Tartar*, about his own nightmarish experiences on the wrong side of Mr Lee's favour, and *Beyond Suspicion? The Singapore Judiciary*. Not surprisingly, none of these books is available in Singapore.

Singapore has been graced by some of Western literature's finest writers. James Clavell's *King Rat*, set in the notorious Japanese POW camp at Changi, JG Farrell's *The Singapore Grip*, set in the same era, and Paul Theroux's rowdy *Saint Jack* are among the most widely read.

The city's cultural commentators have long bemoaned and debated its sparse collection of local literary luminaries, but writers such as the late 'Voice of Singapore' Goh Sin Tub *(Ghosts of Singapore* and *The Ghost Lover of Emerald Hill)*, Philip Jeyaretnam *(Tigers in Paradise, Raffles Place Ragtime)*, Catherine Lim *(The Bondmaid)* and Tan Hwee Hwee *(Mammon Inc)* are well worth reading for insights into how Singapore views itself.

FILMS

Singaporean cinematic achievement in the past has been patchy, to say the least. Lack of money, lack of interest, dearth of creative talent, lack of official encouragement and many other explanations have been cited. Another explanation could be that societies need an underbelly on which cinematic art can feed and, unlike somewhere comparable in size such as Hong Kong, Singapore either lacked that colourful underbelly, or was simply unhappy about the idea of portraying social problems, particularly in a medium with so much power to shape perceptions.

Recently, in line with government efforts to foster a more creative society, money has been poured into local movies, through the conduit of the Singapore Film Commission and local deep-pocket production houses such as Raintree Productions, with mixed success.

The best local director is probably Eric Khoo, whose *Mee Pok Man, 12 Storeys* and *Be With Me* are set in the island's 'heartlands' and have been well received. The latter two were hits at the Cannes Film Festival.

Jack Neo boasts Singapore's three highest-grossing local productions. *Money No Enough* focused on the dark side of the heartlands in the shape of the loan sharks who patrol these vast estates and feed on the impoverished. *I Not Stupid* is an amusing and biting look at Singapore society through its pushy hothouse education system, while the sequel *I Not Stupid Too* was more successful commercially, though not as satirical.

Young director Royston Tan came to prominence in 2005, when his film *15: The Movie*, which dealt with drug abuse and wayward youth, was cut by the censors. As always, the act of censorship won the film more attention and acclaim, making Tan something of a local celebrity, especially after he lampooned the censors in the musical sequence *Cut*. Tan's subsequent efforts, such as the musical comedy *881*, have veered towards the mainstream.

DIRECTORY
TRANSPORT
ARRIVAL & DEPARTURE
AIR

Unless you're coming from Tioman Island (in which case you land at Seletar Airport), all flights arrive at one of the four terminals at **Changi Airport** (☎ 6542 1122, flight information 1800 542 4422; www.changiairport.com), about 20km east of the city centre. There are three main terminals and a Budget Terminal.

Bus

Public bus 36 runs from Terminals 1, 2 and 3 to Orchard Rd and the Colonial District ($1.70, one hour). Buses leave roughly every 15 minutes, the first departing at 6.09am and the last just after midnight.

Faster and more convenient are the airport shuttle buses (adult/child $9/6, 20 to 40 minutes) that leave from all main terminal arrival halls and drop passengers at any hotel, except for those on Sentosa and at Changi Village. They leave from Terminals 1 and 2 and the Budget Terminal (every 30 minutes midnight to 6.15pm, every 15 minutes 6.15pm to midnight) and Terminal 3 (every 15 minutes 6am to 10am and 6pm to 2am, every 30 minutes 11am-6pm and 2am to 6am). Booking desks are in the arrival halls.

Train

The clean and efficient Mass Rapid Transit (MRT) is the best budget way to get into town. The station is located below Terminals 2 and 3, the fare to Raffles Place is $2.70/$1.50 per adult/child (including a $1 refundable deposit) and the journey takes around 35 minutes. You have to change trains at Tanah Merah (just cross the platform). The first train leaves at 5.30am and the last goes at 12.06am.

CLIMATE CHANGE & TRAVEL

Travel – especially air travel – is a significant contributor to global climate change. At Lonely Planet we believe that all who travel have a responsibility to limit their personal impact. As a result we have teamed with Rough Guides and other concerned industry partners to support Climate Care, which allows people to offset the greenhouse gases they are responsible for with contributions to energy-saving projects and other climate-friendly initiatives in the developing world. Lonely Planet offsets all staff and author travel.

For more information, turn to the responsible travel pages on www.lonelyplanet.com. For details on offsetting your carbon emissions and a carbon calculator, go to www.climatecare.org.

Taxi

Taxi lines at Changi are usually fast-moving and efficient, even at the Budget Terminal, and you rarely have to wait long. The fare structure is brain-meltingly complicated, but count on spending anywhere between $18 and $35 into the city centre, depending on the time of travel. The most expensive times are between 5pm and 6am, when a whole smorgasbord of surcharges kick in.

A limousine transfer service operates 24 hours a day and costs a flat $45 to anywhere on the island.

TRAIN

Coming from Malaysia by train, you'll disembark at **Tanjong Pagar Railway Station** (☎ 6222 5165) and may be set upon by taxi touts hoping to take advantage of the absence of a Changi-style controlled system. It's only a kilometre from here into Chinatown, 2km to the Colonial District and 3km to Little India, so the fare should not be more than $10 for the furthest trip. Insist the driver uses the meter or tell him to get lost.

BUS

Buses arriving from Malaysia drop you either at Lavender St Bus Terminal (Map pp84–5, E4), Queen St Terminal (Map pp84–5, D6) or the Golden Mile Complex (p87), all of which are in poor locations

> ### TAKE THE TRAIN
> Travellers concerned with reducing their carbon footprint might consider reaching Singapore overland. Coming from the rest of Southeast Asia, there are train links pretty much all the way from Europe or China (with the exceptions of Cambodia and Laos). A train trip from Chiang Mai to Singapore in standard sleeper carriages only costs around US$80 and takes around three days.

in terms of late-night transport options. Calling a taxi is the best option (see p190).

BOAT

Coming from the Indonesian islands, you'll be disgorged at the **HarbourFront Ferry Terminal** (Map pp130-1, H6; ☎ 6513 2200; www.singaporecruise .com) or at the **Tanah Merah Ferry Terminal** (☎ 6513 2100; www.singapore cruise.com). From HarbourFront, it's a short walk to the HarbourFront MRT station, or there is a taxi rank outside. From Tanah Merah, catch bus 35 to either Bedok or Tanah Merah MRT stations, or catch a taxi.

VISAS

Visitors from the USA, UK, Australia, New Zealand, South Africa, Israel, most European countries and Asean member countries (except Myanmar) receive 30-day tourist visas on arrival by air. Citizens of the

DIRECTORY

Commonwealth of Independent States, Middle Eastern, African and South Asian countries require visas.

CUSTOMS

It's worth noting that visitors are forbidden from bringing cigarettes into Singapore, though in practice few people arriving at the airport are checked. First-time offenders are usually let off with confiscation and a warning.

The limit on alcohol is only 1L of duty-free wine, beer or spirits at the airport (and none if you're arriving from Malaysia or Indonesia), but you can bring as much cash

as you like! Take a letter from your doctor if you carry prescription medication.

Needless to say, it's insane to attempt to bring drugs into Singapore – and there are also strict punishments for bringing in firearms and pornography.

GETTING AROUND

Singapore has fantastic public transport – a tangled web of bus and MRT train routes taking you to the doorstep of most sights. The MRT is easy to navigate, but stops are sometimes far apart (walking in 35°C and high humidity is

Recommended Modes of Transport

	Orchard Rd	Chinatown	Colonial District & the Quays	Little India	Sentosa
Orchard Rd	-	MRT 10min	MRT 5min	MRT 15min	MRT, then monorail 25min
Chinatown	MRT 10min	-	MRT 10min	MRT 15min	MRT, then monorail 15min
Colonial District & the Quays	MRT 5min	MRT 10min	-	MRT 10min	MRT, then monorail 25min
Little India	MRT 15min	MRT 15min	MRT 15min	-	MRT, then monorail 25min
Sentosa	monorail, then MRT 25min	monorail, then MRT 15min	monorail, then MRT 25min	monorail, then MRT 25min	-
Eastern Singapore	bus or MRT 30min	bus or MRT 40min	bus or MRT 30min	bus or MRT 30min	bus or MRT, then monorail 45min
Holland Rd & Bukit Timah	bus 20min	bus 30min	bus 35min	bus 40min	bus 30min
Southwest Singapore	MRT 15min	MRT 5min	MRT 15min	MRT 15min	monorail 5min
Arab Quarter	MRT 10min	MRT 5min	MRT 3min	walk 10min	MRT, then monorail 25min
Jurong	MRT 25min	MRT 35min	MRT 30min	MRT 35min	MRT, then monorail 50min

sweaty work!), so it pays to brush up on those bus routes, which are usually clearly described at bus stops. Pick up a free MRT system map at any MRT station, or the *Bus Guide & Bus Stop Directory* ($3.90) from most bookshops. Due to car-ownership limitations, taxis are also considered public transport.

TRAVEL PASSES

There are two kinds of pass for Singapore public transport that save a whole lot of hassle buying tickets every time you travel.

Buy the Ez-link card from the customer service windows at MRT stations for $15, which includes a $5 nonrefundable deposit. It's good for use on all buses and trains and gives you cheaper fares. The cards can be topped up with cash or ATM cards at station ticket machines.

The **Singapore Tourist Pass** (www .thesingaporetouristpass.com) was finally resurrected after being abandoned for years. It offers unlimited travel on trains and most buses for $8 a day, plus discounts and offers at certain shops and restaurants.

MASS RAPID TRANSIT (MRT)

The ultraclean, safe and efficient Singapore **MRT** (☎ 1800 336 8900;

Eastern Singapore	Holland Rd & Bukit Timah	Southwest Singapore	Arab Quarter	Jurong
MRT or bus 30min	bus 20min	MRT 15min	MRT 10min	MRT 25min
MRT or bus 40min	bus 30min	MRT 5min	MRT 5min	MRT 35min
MRT or bus 30min	bus 35min	MRT 15min	MRT 3min	MRT 30min
MRT or bus 30min	bus 40min	MRT 15min	walk 10min	MRT 35min
monorail, then bus or MRT 45min	monorail, then bus 40min	monorail 5min	MRT, then monorail 25min	MRT, then monorail 50min
-	bus 45min	bus or MRT 35min	MRT or bus 10min	MRT, then bus 1hr
bus 45min	-	bus 30min	bus 40min	bus 35min
MRT or bus 35min	bus 30min	-	bus 30min	bus 35min
MRT or bus 10min	bus 40min	bus 30min	-	MRT 40min
MRT, then bus 1hr	bus 35min	bus 35min	MRT 40min	-

www.smrt.com.sg) subway and light-rail system is the island's pride and joy – or one of them. It's the most comfortable and hassle-free way to get around, not least because it offers an escape from the heat.

Trains run from around 5.30am to just after midnight, departing every three to four minutes at peak times and every six to eight off-peak.

Fares range from $1.10 to $1.90, plus a $1 refundable deposit every time you buy a ticket. Buying an Ez-link card or Tourist Pass (see p189) makes life much easier.

Tickets are available at the automatic machines in stations, which take notes and give change, or from the customer-service windows.

BUS

Singapore's bus service should be the envy of the world. Clean and largely unvandalised, you rarely have to wait very long for one to turn up (but yes, sometimes two turn up at once) and they reach pretty much every corner of the island. Some even have TVs to entertain – or annoy – passengers!

Fares range from $0.90 to $1.80 (10% less with an Ez-link card). When you board the bus, drop the exact money in coins into the fare box (no change is given) or swipe your Ez-link card or Tourist Pass (see p189). Remember to swipe the card again when you get off.

For inquiries contact **SBS Transit** (☎ 1800 287 2727; www.sbstransit.com.sg).

TOURIST BUSES

Singapore Airlines runs the **SIA Hop-On** (☎ 9457 2896; www.siahopon.asiaone.com.sg) tourist bus, traversing the main tourist arteries every 30 minutes daily, starting at Raffles Blvd at 9am, with the last bus leaving at 5.30pm and arriving back at 7.35pm.

There's also a Sentosa Hop-On bus running between Raffles Blvd, Orchard Rd, Lau Pa Sat Festival Market and Sentosa. The first bus leaves Sentosa at 10am and the last at 5.30pm. Tickets cost $12/6 per adult/child, or $3 with a Singapore Airlines or Silk Air boarding pass or ticket. Buy tickets from the driver.

TAXI

The 'taxi issue' is one of Singapore's big unsolvable problems and a constant bugbear and conversation topic for city residents and the media. Sometimes they swarm like locusts, other times there are none, or drivers refuse to stop. Rain showers, peak hours, night-times and shift-change times (which are unpredictable but usually occur between 4pm and 5pm) often render them difficult to find. Getting a taxi home late at night after a night out (especially if you're in a popular zone like the Quays or Orchard Rd) can be a frustrating experience.

The fare structure is enormously complicated, but basically taxis are metered and cost around $2.80 for the first kilometre, then $0.20 for each additional 385m. The average journey within the city centre will cost between $4 and $10, plus surcharges for phone and advance bookings, peak-hour travel and CBD charges.

Credit-card payments incur a 10% surcharge.

If you order a cab by phone you'll be asked your name, location and destination. A message then tells you the licence plate number of your cab and the estimated arrival time.

Taxi company numbers:
Comfort and CityCab CabLink ☎ 6552 1111
Premier Taxis ☎ 6363 6888
SMRT Cabs ☎ 6555 8888

PRACTICALITIES
BUSINESS HOURS
Shops generally open late and close late, so don't bother heading to Orchard Rd at 9am to beat the crowd – virtually nothing will be open until at least 10am, but shops will stay open until 9pm and often later.

Restaurants usually close between 2pm and 5pm, but hawker centres keep the woks on all day and often late into the night.

Government office hours are generally 9am to 6pm Monday to Friday, and 10am to 1pm on Saturday.

DISCOUNTS
Children receive up to 50% discount at most tourist venues, sometimes gauged by how tall they are rather than by age. They can ride the MRT for free if they're under 90cm tall. Students with ID cards receive discounts at some venues.

ELECTRICITY
Electricity supply is reliable and runs at 220V to 240V and 50 cycles. Plugs are of the three-pronged, square-pin type used in the UK.

EMERGENCIES
Singapore has a very low crime rate and members of both sexes can walk around safely at any time of night. Pickpockets sometimes target tourists and the odd gang fight makes front-page news, but unless you go looking for it, trouble is unlikely to come looking for you. Don't import, take or sell drugs in Singapore or hang out with anyone who does – the death penalty awaits.
Ambulance/Fire ☎ 995
Police ☎ 999
SOS Helpline ☎ 1800 774 5935

Hospitals with 24-hour accident and emergency departments:

Gleneagles Hospital (Map pp40–1, C3; ☎ 6470 5688; 6A Napier Rd)

Mt Elizabeth Hospital (Map pp40–1, F3; ☎ 6731 2218; 3 Mt Elizabeth Rd)

Raffles Hospital (Map pp68–9, G1; ☎ 6311 1111; 585 North Bridge Rd)

Singapore General Hospital (Map pp52–3, A4; ☎ 6321 4113; Level 2, Block 1, Outram Rd)

HOLIDAYS

New Year's Day 1 January

Chinese New Year January/February (two days); date varies based on lunar calendar.

Good Friday April

Labour Day 1 May

Vesak Day May; varies.

National Day 9 August

Hari Raya Puasa October/November; date varies based on Islamic calendar.

Deepavali October; date varies according to the Indian almanac.

Christmas Day 25 December

Hari Raya Haji December/January; date varies based on Islamic calendar.

INTERNET

Most internet cafes in Singapore are actually gaming centres, so things can get raucous. However, most tend to be bereft of teenagers and OK for a Skype call during school hours. Nearly all hotels provide internet access, both in the form of wi-fi or wired in-room connections as well as in business centres. Changi Airport has dozens of free internet terminals.

SingTel (www.singtel.com.sg) and **StarHub** (www.starhub.com) are the two biggest local providers of wireless, and you can buy cards allowing wireless access at most convenience stores.

Singapore has an ever-expanding network of around 1000 wi-fi hotspots – and most cafes and pubs operate them. A list of hotspots can be found by following the Wireless@sg link at www.infocomm123.sg.

Some useful and interesting websites:

Changi International Airport (www.changi.airport.com.sg) Flight information and services at the world's favourite airport. Try to locate the free swimming pool.

Go There Singapore (http://gothere.sg) For sheer usefulness, it would be hard to beat this site, which will help you locate anything in Singapore.

Hungry Go Where (www.hungrygowhere.com) Independent reviews of everything from hawker stalls to restaurants in the Lion City.

Mr Brown (www.mrbrown.com) Website of blogger and podcaster Lee Kin Mun, who gained wider fame when his column in the *Today* newspaper was canned after he wrote rather too frankly about rising living costs in Singapore.

Singapore Government (www.gov.sg) As you'd expect, very large and very comprehensive.

Singapore Tourism Board (www.visitsingapore.com) Information on the city's top attractions, plus a useful events calendar.

Stomp (www.stomp.com.sg) Community site run by the official mouthpiece media company SPH, embodying the kind of carefully monitored 'open society' the government is trying to foster (pictures of people kissing in clubs and 'hot' teacher contests, but nothing too dangerous). For an insight into issues that preoccupy Singaporeans, check the 'Singapore Seen' section.

LANGUAGE

Singapore's official languages are Malay, Mandarin, Tamil and English.

Nearly everyone speaks Singapore's baffling English patois, known proudly as Singlish, which most visitors will find extremely hard to understand. Singlish is essentially an English dialect mixed with Hokkien, Malay and Tamil, spoken in a rapid, staccato fashion – sentences are polished off with innumerable but essentially meaningless exclamatory words – *lah* is the most common, but you'll also hear *mah, lor, meh, leh, hor* and several others. (We once overheard a boy delivering the dubious romantic overture 'I love you *hor*' to his girlfriend.)

Fortunately for the bewildered visitor, most Singaporeans will instantly switch seamlessly into a more standardised English when they are speaking to foreigners, though if you have a strong accent yourself, don't be surprised if it's they who find you incomprehensible.

MONEY

If you use the MRT and buses, eat and drink at hawker centres and stay in budget accommodation, it's possible to get by in Singapore on less than $50 a day. Staying in a midrange hotel, eating in a mix of venues and doing some modest shopping will send your costs up above $200. Count on around $300 to $400 a day for a pleasantly indulgent stay. For exchange rates, see the Quick Reference (inside front cover).

NEWSPAPERS & MAGAZINES

The press in Singapore is theoretically free to assert its opinions, but in reality this is far from the case. Willing self-censorship combines with stern government oversight and complicit editors to keep dissent away from the pages of the local press.

The country's flagship paper is the *Straits Times* broadsheet, which will likely strike readers from places with more vibrant newspapers as being more than just a little on the tame side. The paper's coverage of Asia is not bad, though it's also skewed towards reinforcing national interests. The tabloid *New Paper* offers up a lurid platter of crime, scandal, sensation and English football.

International English-language publications such as *Time* and *Newsweek* are readily available, but you won't find the *Far Eastern Economic Review,* which has been banned and sued for daring to publish a story about opposition leader Chee Soon Juan. Malaysian newspapers are similarly restricted from sale (the ban is reciprocated in Malaysia on Singaporean papers).

Although there are plenty of lurid-looking magazines on the racks, pornography (including relatively tame publications such as *Playboy* and *Penthouse*) is prohibited. Some magazines, such as *Cosmopolitan*, are available – though note the 'Parental Warning' label stuck on the cover.

For entertainment listings, see *8 Days, Time Out* or *I-S* magazines. Lifestyle magazines include *Her World* and *Expat Living*. Gourmands should check out *Tatler's Singapore's Best Restaurants* guide, while hawker-food enthusiasts should buy the excellent *Makansutra* guidebook for an encyclopaedic rundown of the city's best street food, with a decent restaurant section as well.

ORGANISED TOURS

A number of companies offer tours that promise to reveal a different side to the city, or go into more depth about a certain aspect of Singapore culture. Some good ones:

Betel Box Tours (☎ 6247 7340; www .betelbox.com) Tony Tan (p109) and the Betel Box team lead a variety of tours around Singapore, from bicycling to nature walks. Undoubtedly the coolest for the gourmand is the Thursday night food walk, in which Tony himself gets travellers to experience the best of Joo Chiat's culinary offers and social history.

Imperial Cheng Ho Dinner Cruise (☎ 6533 9811; www.watertours.com.sg; daytime & dinner cruises adult $27-55, child $14-29) Cruises around Singapore waters in a hulking old replica of the *Cheng Ho* junk.

Original Singapore Walks (☎ 6325 1631; www.singaporewalks.com; adult/child from $25/15) Superb and deservedly popular series of offbeat guided walks through various parts of the city, including Chinatown, Little India and the quays, as well as WWII tours. No booking necessary, just check the website for meeting times and turn up.

Singapore DUCK Tours (☎ 6333 3825; www.ducktours.com.sg; adult/child $33/17) A bright yellow amphibious vehicle that tours the city streets before plunging into the harbour. We're including this because never again are you likely to have a chance to be so comprehensively embarrassed.

TELEPHONE

Singaporeans enjoy some of the cheapest mobile phone rates in Asia, and, as getting a local SIM card for your own mobile takes about 10 minutes at any mobile phone store (you'll need to bring your passport), getting a local number is a good investment if you're planning on using your mobile in Singapore even a few times. Should you use your own mobile number roaming charges will apply, but as Singapore's two cell phone networks (GSM900 and GSM1800) make it compatible with most of the rest of the world you'll still be in business. Keep in mind that certain areas – mostly along the coast of East Coast Park – Indonesia's signal may push into Singapore's 'airspace', so your calls will be routed through Indonesia – a potentially costly detour!

USEFUL PHONE NUMBERS

Local Directory Inquiries ☎ 100
International Direct Dial Code ☎ 001
International Directory Inquiries ☎ 104
International Operator ☎ 1635
Singapore International Dial Code ☎ 65
Toll-free Tourist Hotline ☎ 1800 736 2000
Weather ☎ 6542 7788

TIPPING

Tipping is largely unnecessary and unexpected in restaurants because of the 10% service charge automatically added to your bill. Some restaurants voluntarily omit the charge. You aren't expected to tip in hawker centres (indeed, you would be looked upon oddly if you did) or in taxis. Tipping after a massage isn't a bad idea.

TOURIST INFORMATION

Singapore Tourism Board (STB; ☎ 1800 736 2000; www.visitsingapore.com) provides the widest range of services, including tour bookings and event ticketing. There are visitors centres at the following locations (note Suntec City is an unstaffed info desk).
Changi Airport (Terminals 1, 2 & 3; ⏱ 6am-2am)
HarbourFront (Map pp130–1, H6; 01-31D, HarbourFront Centre; ⏱ 10am-6pm)
Liang Court (Map pp68–9, C4; Level 1, Liang Court Shopping Centre, 177 River Valley Rd; ⏱ 10am-10pm)
Orchard Rd (Map pp40–1, G4; Cnr Cairnhill & Orchard Rds; ⏱ 9.30am-10.30pm)
Suntec City (Map pp68–9, G4; Level 1, Suntec City, 3 Temasek Blvd, ⏱ 10am-6pm)

TRAVELLERS WITH DISABILITIES

Most major hotels, shopping malls and tourist attractions have good wheelchair access, but Little India's and Chinatown's crowded narrow footpaths will challenge anyone with mobility, sight or hearing issues. Taxis are plentiful, the MRT is wheelchair-friendly and Singaporeans are happy to help out. We've used the disabled icon to indicate venues with disabled access.

Access Singapore (www.dpa.org .sg) is a useful guidebook for the disabled, available free from the website and STB offices (see above).

>INDEX

See also separate subindexes for See (p204), Shop (p205), Eat (p206), Drink (p207) and Play (p207).

◎ SEE

INDEX

000 map pages